AUSTIN HEALING
Cautionary Tales From 20 Years of South By Southwest

by Oliver Gray

Published by Sarsen Press
© Oliver Gray 2024

Cover design and layout by Richard Williams
Ed Sheeran photo by Michelle Stuart

Contact Oliver Gray at www.olivergray.com

ISBN:978-1-3999-9446-0

Printed and bound by CPI Group UK Ltd, Croydon, CR0 4YY

ACKNOWLEDGEMENTS

Grateful thanks to the following for help and encouragement:

Birgit Gray, Paul Dominy, Rich Williams, Tony Hill, Tim Jones, Paul Kerr, Geoff Wall, Tony Hill and most of all, Elizabeth Derczo, without whom none of it would have been possible.

CONTENTS

FRONT COVER

From top left

2003: Peter Bruntnell and James Walbourne
2004: Black Keys (Dan Auerbach)
2005: Graham Coxon
2006: Mark Mallman
2007: Amy Winehouse
2008: Luke Doucet
2009: Bobby Gillespie
2010: Band Of Skulls (Emma Richardson)
2011: Susanna Hoffs
2012: Jimmy Cliff
2013: Debbie Harry
2014: Andrew Combs and the Kernal
2015: Marlon Williams
2016: Jason Lytle
2017: Jesse Dayton
2018: Courtney Marie Andrews
2019: Arthur Brown
2020: Como Las Movies
2021: Chuck Prophet
2022: Low Cut Connie (Adam Weiner)

FOREWORD

"What is it REALLY like?" That's the question my friends ask me about SXSW. "It's impossible to describe", is always my answer. Not that that has stopped me from trying to do just that, in twenty years' worth of reviews for seven different magazines. This book draws all those articles together and adds a bit of history, some extra annotations, a bunch of 'venue focuses' and rather too many admissions of inadequacy and vulnerability.

The book also describes a unique and special friendship that has been sustained throughout two decades of music appreciation.

So here's what it's REALLY like.

INKY JOURNO

Tin Pan Alley, they call it. I'm not sure of the derivation of the expression, but it must be to do with percussion. Denmark Street in London has long been the heart and soul of the music industry and any visit to it before its redevelopment to make way for Crossrail meant a plunge deep into an environment which lived and breathed music - not unlike the South By Southwest Festival in Texas, in fact.

For me, any visit to Denmark Street would normally take place on the way from Waterloo Station to a gig at one of the iconic venues off Tottenham Court Road, such as The Astoria or the much-loved Borderline, whose line-up of roots and Americana music could easily be taken from any showcases at SXSW. A wander down Denmark Street would entail encounters with places of legend. The proliferation of recording studios and music shops meant that many well-known artists were to be found here back in the sixties, perusing 'Musicians Wanted' notices. Elton John recorded here and it's even alleged that David Bowie lived briefly in a converted ambulance on the street. Pete Townshend bought gear from Macari's guitar shop and The Who rehearsed at Regent Sound, where the Rolling Stones also recorded their third single Not Fade Away. At number 5 was Top Gear, where guitarists like Jimmy Page, Eric Clapton and Hank Marvin would buy their equipment. Bob Marley bought his Les Paul, which had previously belonged to Marc Bolan, from there. I picture the whole scene to be like some kind of musical Tower Of Babel, with sounds emitting from every doorway.

I personally associate Denmark Street with thoughts of my guitar and sartorial hero Tony Hicks of the Hollies. This band had scores of hits all over the world but few of them came from their own pens. Tony Hicks, however, displayed a talent for finding and choosing songs that would work for the band by trawling the offices of the music publishers that lined Tin Pan Alley in the 60s, 70s and 80s. Here he found songs like Here I Go Again, Look Through Any Window, I'm Alive and many of their other hits.

When I interviewed the Hollies in Norwich in 1971, it was a tense encounter. I had just begun to lose faith in them and they were at the absolute nadir of their career as far as I was concerned. Graham Nash had left to go to America, they'd made a ghastly LP of Bob Dylan covers and had abandoned their tie-die hippie togs in favour of hideous white suits and bow ties. But oh joy, I was able to achieve the biggest scoop I ever attained as a music journalist: "I've found a new song that we're going to record. I'm sure it's going to be as big a hit as A Whiter Shade Of Pale", enthused Tony. Sure enough, just weeks later, He Ain't Heavy, He's My Brother was released and became a massive hit.

In more recent days, the Sex Pistols famously lived and rehearsed at 6-7 Denmark Street. According to legend, Glen Matlock saw an advert for the rehearsal space, inserted by someone who used to manage Badfinger, and Malcolm McLaren promised to pay him lots of money to rent it, although it's unknown whether he actually stumped up. A mural, featuring not only McLaren but also Sid Vicious and Nancy Spungeon, was drawn by Johnny Rotten on the walls of Number 6-7, which dates back to the 17th century. A listed building under the protection of Historic England, the house is now one of the many musical instrument shops in Denmark Street.

My friend, the record producer Richard Mazda, was the manager of an extraordinary Denmark Street venue called the Twelve Bar, in character not unlike some of the 'dive' bars of Texas. That place was so small that if you ascended the steps to the tiny balcony you could look down upon the heads of the musicians below. The capacity was an uncomfortable fifty people and you had to fight your way through the narrow front bar in order to get there.

But why am I starting a book about a Texan music festival in a scruffy street in London? Well, it's because my journey to SXSW started there in Denmark Street. At number 4 was an iconic bookshop called Helter Skelter, which sold only music books and was also the headquarters of a music book publishing company of the same name. Its creator and owner was a charming, modest and quiet person by the name of Sean Body. Alongside the daily running of the shop, Sean himself was also an author, creating one of the most intriguing and readable books of the genre in the form of Wish The World Away, a detailed history of the San Francisco band American Music Club.

When I made my first foray into music book publication with a memoir called Volume in the year 2000, I didn't even know of the existence of Helter Skelter, but a friend drew my attention to them and suggested I might ask them to stock it. This led to a visit to Sean, who gave me much encouragement and many useful tips, as well as agreeing to stock the book. During my visit, I was almost tempted into buying an enormous tome about Led Zeppelin, simply because it mentioned the name Andrew Johns, someone who I had been at school with in the 1960s and who went on to become an enormously successful record producer.

Also on the shelves at Helter Skelter was a range of music magazines, many of which I had never come across, because of their non-availability in mainstream newsagents' shops. One of these was an American publication called Amplifier. Not having a particular interest in amplifiers, I almost overlooked it, but a brief leaf-through revealed that, rather than a technical handbook, it was a wide-ranging and professional-looking music magazine, not unlike the UK's Mojo, Select and Q. It was a glossy colour publication, not a fanzine, and its musical emphasis appeared to be Americana, psych and power pop - pretty much mirroring my own musical tastes.

When I got home, a little idea wormed its way into my head. I remembered the days of the music 'inkies', the weekly newspapers that tended to come out on Thursdays or Fridays with names like Sounds, Melody Maker, Record Mirror and NME. Most of them had their own US correspondents, sent out to New York or LA and establishing what they would charmingly call a 'bureau', in order to cover the latest goings-on in the American music industry. Nowadays it seems incredible that the finance could ever have existed for such an indulgence, but as far as I was concerned, this would have been the ultimate in dream jobs.

Now I need to provide a brief summary of my own career in music journalism. Far away from writers like Chris Charlesworth and Sylvie Simmons in their American bureaux, I began writing about music in the early seventies while studying at the University of East Anglia in Norwich, an establishment at which music played a prominent role. During my time there I was able, for the weekly student paper, to interview artists such as Marc Bolan, Free, Joe Cocker, Pink Floyd, Fairport Convention, Jeff Lynne in his band The Idle Race and many more. This was how (see above) I came to interview my original heroes The Hollies.

What I should have done on leaving university was follow the example of the likes of Allan Jones and other brave music writers and decamp to London in the hope of getting work on one of the inkies, but I was far too timid and ended up, inevitably, in the teaching profession. A few forays into reviews and interviews while working in Germany gave me the idea, having established myself in a teaching job in Winchester, UK, to approach the local newspaper in 1977 and ask if they would like someone to write about all the music going on in the area. It scarcely seems possible now, but the elderly proprietor of the local weekly paper, the Hampshire Chronicle, immediately allocated me my own monthly column and gave me completely free range to write about anything musical happening locally, apart, of course, from classical music, which already had its own column. This led to a residency on that paper that lasted over twenty years and allowed me to review and interview hundreds of artists, spanning eras from Prog to Punk to Rock to Metal to New

Wave and beyond. What was more, there were so many acres of newsprint to fill that I wasn't even given a word limit to adhere to. This enabled enormous levels of verbosity, which was a fashionable style at the time.

It was less ambition and more sheer vanity that decreed that this level of independence and access was not enough for me. I was still steamingly jealous of all those cool London scribes who had their much more trendy outlets on the inky weeklies, so I strove to get in with those publications as well. In summary, the results were not sensational: I ended up with zero contributions to Melody Maker, one single contribution to NME, two contributions to Sounds and a year or so of reviewing live bands for the less-fashionable Record Mirror.

This was not exactly a stellar writing career, but below the well-known papers was another stratum of frankly inferior ones, and here was where I found my home, first at a paper called Musicians Only, to which I contributed almost every week for several years before it closed down. This was surely not a coincidence, as the same fate befell the other two second-tier inkies for whom I subsequently worked, Musicians Weekly Classified and the almost plagiaristically-titled Soundmaker. I think the reading figures for these weekly publications must have been minuscule, but they did give me access to the Holy Grail of all reviewers, namely free admission to gigs and backstage passes.

In addition to all this, plus of course a full-time teaching job, I couldn't resist getting involved in numerous local publications with names such as Night Out, Venue, Sound Info and Due South, the last of which was actually a high-quality music, arts and lifestyle magazine that lasted for a good number of years in the Southampton area.

So there I was in Helter Skelter, perusing the pages of Amplifier magazine, which appeared to be published from somewhere in Massachusetts, and noting that it had a strong emphasis on UK bands but seemingly didn't have any UK writers. Maybe, at last, I could fulfil a dream of becoming UK correspondent for an American publication with my very own 'bureau' at home in Winchester? With this in mind, I posted off a copy of the newly published Volume book to the address listed in the magazine, with little hope of any response.

In the event, all my hopes were exceeded, as Amplifier's editor Joe Joyce published a very positive review of the book and, unsolicited by me, asked if I would be willing to become its UK correspondent. Of course, as with 90 percent of my writing, there would be no financial reward involved, but it was an offer which someone with my level of vanity could not possibly resist. My ambitions far exceeded my actual abilities, but it meant that I now had an outlet to a much bigger audience than the readers of the Hampshire Chronicle.

While still firmly in the minor league of music writing, I was nonetheless in a particularly fertile period, because I also had two other, albeit unlikely, outlets. It was the time when, as the Inkies had entered what was to become a terminal decline, but no internet reporting existed in any significant form, other outlets were available. Foremost among these was a full-colour A5 magazine called The Fly. Owned by a small chain of Fly-branded venues that lasted a few years before being swallowed up by bigger conglomerates, The Fly was conceived primarily as a listings magazine for gigs, but it also contained numerous articles, photos and interviews with current 'buzz' bands, some carried out by reporters from the Inkies.

The Fly was generously distributed free to hundreds of small venues all round the UK. I remember a cardboard box would arrive every month at Winchester's Railway Inn venue, where I promoted gigs, containing hundreds of copies of The Fly, the vast majority of which would be dumped, unread, into the recycling bin when the next month's issue arrived. Personally, I read it avidly, but no one else seemed to. I surmised that maybe they printed those vast numbers of copies so that they could claim huge circulation figures in order to entice advertisers.

The Fly certainly didn't look like a template that would inspire imitations, but oddly enough, it did. It has always seemed strange to me that many people choose to base businesses on doing exactly the same as something already being done by someone else, but a businessman in Southampton decided to produce a magazine that was virtually the same as The Fly. Entitled LOGO, its format was identical but slightly plusher, printed on higher quality paper, but it was a monthly music magazine in the same format, and distributed free. Maybe the owner was enticed by those just-mentioned advertisers and their potential cash, or maybe he was as idealistic as he claimed to be, motivated by wanting to offer exposure to aspiring musicians. Who knew, but it was perfect for me as the local music-writing bod, keen to broaden my horizons.

LOGO looked, and indeed was, a credible publication, and before long I was enthusiastically churning out articles and interviews for it, once even travelling to Brussels to interview the Californian band Grandaddy, one of my favourites. This was a particularly gruelling experience, since I was really only interested in front-man and songwriter Jason Lytle, but despite comprehensive arrangements having been made beforehand, he was unable (or unwilling) to be interviewed. I ended up having to interview the keyboard player who, having not written any of the songs, was unable to answer any of my carefully-prepared questions about their lyrical content. On top of that, I got thrown out of the venue after knocking a full glass of the very potent Belgian lager I was drinking off a balcony, drenching the customers below. Still, an article of sorts was forthcoming, and LOGO lasted a couple of years before collapsing in disarray. Produced in the seedy rooms above Southampton's famous Joiners Arms venue, LOGO's demise came when the landlord, peering into a filing cabinet, was shocked to find that LOGO had a secret sideline in the form of … how should I put this? … porn. This was presumably more profitable than the magazine, as it rarely carried any advertising at all and had no visible means to cover its doubtless expensive production costs.

Up in Winchester, an arguably even more extraordinary publication was germinating. Based firmly on that same principle of convincing advertisers of its vast circulation, the Mid-Hampshire Observer was one of a small stable of local 'free weeklies' in newspaper format.

Page after page of advertising sat alongside local news stories and conversation points. Once again, there was actually no need for this paper to exist, because there already was a Winchester free sheet, but The Observer was a very different kettle of fish. Somehow, in a masterstroke that I've never really fully understood, it had been taken over editorially by a bunch of super-hip young writers with their roots in local arts organisations and bands. These included Pete Harvey and Richard Williams, both cool customers who had been in a signed band called Trip and were very active in the local music scene.

With seemingly no one in authority to curb its excesses, the Observer had pages of editorial to fill with anything they felt like writing about. I knew that virtually no one actually read it. How did I know that? Because I could see it each week in the local Tesco store, where a pile of these papers would be stacked near the exit for people to help themselves, and be replaced, virtually untouched, the following week, just like The Fly in the Railway. I also knew it because I wrote scores of pages for the Observer but no one ever mentioned any of the often controversial articles to me at all, and reader feedback was virtually non-existent. But as an outlet, it was just fantastic, because I could indulge my most excessive Lester Bangs delusions, as indeed did all the other writers.

Cynicism reigned at The Observer, as pseudo-intellectual references, in-jokes, outrageous double-meaning headlines and left-of-centre politics filled the pages of this unique, unforgettable publication. A visit to their offices always made me feel part of something that must have been akin to the smoke-filled rooms of the London Inkies. It was an incredible era that ended in sadness, as the chief reporter was killed in a car accident and the devastated colleagues never really recovered. Eventually the staff all moved on to more conventional jobs, but a version of The Mid-Hants Observer still lives on, albeit with no editorial content at all. Me, I profited by being able to make the true claim that my work was regularly appearing in 'The Observer', which strictly speaking was true, just not in the sense in which it was sometimes taken.

WHY?

First published in my 2001 book VACATION,
this chapter describes my first visit to Austin, Texas.

That idea of the cacophony, the musical Tower of Babel that I imagined Denmark Street to be, was eventually experienced for the first time on Sixth Street in Austin, Texas, in 1999. I had read so much about the city described (by itself) as the Music Capitol (sic) of the USA, that I finally decided I had to experience it myself, and persuaded my endlessly tolerant wife Birgit to accompany me.

The question we were asked again and again before, during and after our visit to Austin, was "Why?" But I knew all about Austin, I thought.

Down in Southampton, there's a music club called The Brook. There I had seen artists such as Omar and the Howlers, Joe Ely and Bobby Mack. What they all had in common was that they all came from Texas and they all shared a thwacking blues-rock style after the fashion of Austin's acknowledged musical hero Stevie Ray Vaughan. Apart, that is, from poor Bobby Mack, who complained that he couldn't get a gig in Austin.

Couldn't get a gig in Austin? How so? It is a city that contains hundreds of live music venues, far more per square mile than anywhere else on the planet. If a fine guitar player such as Bobby Mack couldn't get a gig there, then what must the quality control be like? I was worried, I'll admit it. The 'Why?' definitely seemed to suggest that Austin must be grotty by day and of no interest to anyone not into music. Was it going to be unsuitable as a holiday destination, as opposed to a research object or an anorak's delight?

We arrived at Houston airport and suffered an immediate embarrassment when we couldn't start the hire car. Apparently, you can't start an automatic when it's in gear, but how were we to know that? But we got it going and as we cruised the highway (that sounds so great, I'll say it again: cruised the highway) towards Austin, I imagined a road movie-style motel rearing up out of the heat haze, where we would chew the fat with the local cowboys and stick a dime into the jukebox. However, the perfect motel somehow never seemed to appear, so Birgit just had to keep driving ... and driving ... and driving. The problem was that she was severely jetlagged and getting more and more tired. As her eyelids began to droop irrevocably, there was good news, as a sign appeared declaring: Austin City Limits.

I took out a map of the city and tried to orientate myself. It seemed perfectly straightforward. We were on the main highway through Austin, Interstate 35, and to either side stretched the various roads: First Street, Second Street, Third Street, etc. How straightforward. All we had to do was drive down one of these and there was bound to be a hotel where we could stay. The only trouble was that we were up in the air on an elevated freeway, while the roads on the map were down below. As I haplessly tried to interpret the map, the trouble started.

We descended on a slip road, but before we knew it, we found ourselves heading off back down Highway 35 towards San Antonio. The exhausted Birgit was beginning to get angry. Off we came again, only to disappear into a massive trading estate full of warehouses, fast food outlets and furniture stores but no hotels. Back onto the freeway, off it again, down a few dead-ends, onto another freeway heading north towards Dallas, off it again ...

Suddenly, as in a scene from a movie, Birgit pulled onto the sidewalk, threw open the door, tossed the keys into my lap, shouted, "That's it, you can bloody drive yourself, I've had enough!", slammed the door shut again and took off down the road on foot.

Phew! I love you when you're angry! This was quite a sensational moment, not at all the way she normally behaves, but pretty damn impressive. People always do that in road movies, don't they? How authentic! But I have a well-documented driving phobia, so there was nothing for it but to trot off down the road after her, gesticulating, grovellingly apologising for my uselessness and begging for clemency. "I'll pay for us to stay in the smartest hotel in town," I heard myself saying, unconvincingly.

"Sod off. I don't want the smartest hotel, I want the nearest hotel, you idiot."

The nearest hotel turned out to be a La Quinta, just round the corner. It only had a Smoking room left, but Birgit was beyond caring and I was beyond daring (to suggest trying to find another hotel). She collapsed onto the bed and passed out, but something peculiar had happened to me. I was wide awake and raring to check out this paradise I'd come so far to experience. Oh, and there was another thing.

In the plane on the way over, I'd been reading the biography of Billy Bragg. This singer and songwriter appealed to me in the way that Tony Benn and Ken Livingstone did, in that he's a realistic socialist whose every word seems to make total sense. Plus, he has a perhaps unexpectedly well-developed sense of humour.

On my headphones on the plane, I was listening to a brilliant album called Mermaid Avenue that Billy had made with a Chicago band called Wilco, re-interpreting the songs of Woody Guthrie. But, as I listened, something even more remarkable happened. The magazine had a section on Austin, which revealed that Billy Bragg was appearing that very day, at somewhere called Waterloo.

Probably my only positive characteristic in life is a determination to carry out tasks which I set myself. And there, on the plane, I had set myself the task of seeing Billy Bragg at Waterloo in Austin, Texas. I could not possibly imagine anything better. And I couldn't imagine not achieving it.

It was mid-evening and the heat was stifling as, sleepless, I left the La Quinta and strode down the steep hill towards Sixth Street. In the distance, sounds were becoming apparent: the thwack of a snare drum, the rumble of a bass, the chunky chiming of a Telecaster. But then, there seemed to be more than one of each, coming from all directions. As I reached Sixth, I realised that the myth was, in fact, reality: Every building in the street was a bar, and every bar had a band playing in it. Ooh, it was the dream I had had of what Denmark Street must have been like in days of old.

Admittedly, I was jet-lagged, but I certainly wasn't on drugs. I had never felt as wonderful as I did in that moment. If you can't relate to music, it doesn't matter. Just think of your favourite thing in the world, be it art, literature, sport, food, religion or whatever, then imagine yourself completely surrounded and engulfed by it. There, doesn't that feel good?

On the corner was a brightly-lit bar. The band was taking a break, so I approached the girl who was serving:

"Excuse me, do you know where Billy Bragg is playing?"

"Who?"

"Billy Bragg."

"Just a moment ... Wayne, do you know where Bobby Bland is playing?"

"No, no ... hang on ... How can I get to Waterloo?"

"Oh, that's easy. Just keep on walking down Sixth and you'll get there soon enough."

It was eleven o'clock at night but something like five in the morning for me. I didn't care. On and on I walked, occasionally stopping to get a reassuring "Just keep right on walking", until, after at least two miles, I saw a neon sign depicting the word Waterloo in the format of the London Undergound sign graphic at the top of a hill. This was it!

Except that it wasn't. Waterloo turned out to be a record shop, not a club. What was more, Billy Bragg had been there at lunchtime, merely performing a couple of songs and doing a CD signing session. And none of the staff I spoke to seemed remotely interested in either Billy or his work. Still, the journey hadn't been wasted. I felt that I had done my duty, so bought a couple of CDs and set off back the way I had come. On the return journey, I visited five bars, had five beers, heard five bands and ate the most heavenly hamburger of my life, all at (for me) breakfast time.

During the next few days, we found that just wandering around was a fine occupation in Austin. Mainly because the University of Texas campus is so gigantic and the population so youthful, it is one of the USA's least threatening cities. Most appealingly, we found that it had a number of large urban parks. One of these surrounded the newly-restored State Capitol, a beautiful pink, domed building from where the state of Texas is governed. It was worth entering just for a cool-down. When we were in Austin, the outside temperature was 95 degrees and walking into the State Capitol was literally like leaping from a sauna into a splashpool (except that, thankfully, everyone kept their clothes on). It was worth trying out the startling amplifying effect of speaking below the four-floor high dome. Most sounds in Austin are amplified ones.

On an incline just outside the city centre, we found Zilker Park, a joyous destination on a hot day because of its freshwater spring-fed lake, Barton Springs. For a mere three bucks, we could spend the day slipping in and out of the crystal-clear 68 degree waters and soaking up the sun on the grass slopes. Most of the clientèle was exquisitely tattooed and comprehensively body-pierced, so our lily-white British hue elicited plenty of "Why Austin?"s and much in the way of friendly and welcoming banter. Afterwards, we sauntered through the Botanical gardens and took a ride on the Zilker Zephyr miniature railway.

After leaving the emergency hotel, the accommodation we found was mind-bogglingly good. Long before the days of Airbnb, the annexe we were allotted turned out to be a separate colonial-style house, complete with its own veranda and rocking chair, a huge fan-cooled sitting room, a large kitchen with a fully-stocked 'help yourself to ice cream' fridge-freezer and a bedroom of unparalleled luxury - all for the price of a standard motel. Breakfast was a gourmet feast of fresh fruit and a different speciality delight each day, including home-made spinach quiche and 'Texan Egg Florets'

- poached eggs and herbs in a choux pastry basket.

So, about that music ... How could it have disappointed? The only problem lay in deciding which bars to enter and how long to stay. We could have plied Sixth for weeks before repeating ourselves, but we found that it was best to be adventurous, stick a pin in the huge listings guide in the Austin Chronicle and take a flyer on someone we hadn't heard of. You certainly weren't going to be disappointed by the quality.

The premier club in Austin was Antone's, a huge blues cavern. It was so full that they had set up little satellite bars on wheels out in the audience to relieve the crush at the main bars. These fairy-light-adorned bathtubs full of ice and bottled beer rapidly sold out and had to be frequently replenished. We caught the third night in an annual four-night residency by the legendary James Brown saxist Maceo Parker and his impossibly funky band. According to the people we talked to, the whole of Austin looks forward to Maceo's visits, which explained why the eighty-dollar tickets were so hard to come by.

As we queued, the band rolled up outside the club in a fleet of limos with darkened windows. We danced until 2 am before retiring in exhaustion while Maceo played on. As with everywhere we went, we made friends instantly, always based on the inevitable "Why Austin?" In this case, the reply was easy: "Just look around you. Isn't it obvious?"

It would be easy to drone on about all the rest of the music, but we felt that even non-music freaks should visit Austin for the stunningly beautiful surrounding countryside. We found a quick way to sample its appeal by taking a half-hour drive out to the Austinites' favourite excursion destination, the Oasis on Lake Travis. This precariously-perched eight-storey wooden hillside construction houses a whole range of restaurants and bars from which we could peer over the balcony railing (28 decks, 450 feet above the water) and savour what was claimed to be the world's most spectacular sunset (I wouldn't argue, but then I haven't been everywhere in the world), whilst dining surprisingly reasonably.

Back in Austin, the old problem raised itself: So many venues, so little time. Pin-sticking in the Chronicle proved triumphant once more, as the unpromising-sounding Monte Montgomery at the even less enticing-sounding Saxon Pub, turned out to be a feast of brilliant self-penned acoustic country-rock in a classic Texas roadhouse setting. We banged down a few Tequilas, bought Monte's album and shouted "Yeah!' a lot. At the time of writing, nearly a quarter of a century later, Monte still regularly plays at the Saxon Pub.

A FRIEND INDEED

I first met Paul Dominy under musical circumstances that were created by my writing activity. I was in charge of Live Reviews for the south of England for the minor-league inky Musicians Only, and always on the lookout for good local bands to encourage. Because the paper was designed mainly for musicians (the clue was in the title) the Live Reviews came in a format which required the reviewer to list all the gear the bands used - what brands of amps, guitars, drum kits etc. This meant that it was essential to talk either to band members or some member of the road crew to gather the information.

One day in August 1980, Birgit was away and I had nothing to do, so I scanned the NME Gig Guide listings to find a local band and spotted that an outfit called The Time was playing in a small pub called The Plough in Durrington, on Salisbury Plain. It didn't sound particularly promising but I had nothing else to do, so turned up at this very unlikely venue. The first thing I saw was the support band. They were called, rather tastelessly I thought, Paschendale, and all of them had black leather jackets with their band name embossed on the back. They creaked as they walked around and they actually looked slightly intimidating, in contrast to The Time who, despite their youthful, punky image, had a friendly and humorous aura. It's strange to think that I have been in touch with all of them ever since. Phil the bassist is now a thatcher and lives near us. Tweets, the hedgehog-like guitarist, leads a covers band that plays regularly in our area. The drummer Chris lives near my son-in-law's childhood home in Gosport and lead singer Kevin Robinson is now much better known as the ubiquitous comedian and character actor Kevin Eldon.

My job, however, was to home in on the sound engineer, a small, skinny person, crowned with a peroxide hair-do clearly modelled on Sting, and presiding over a gigantic sound desk that took up much of the room. I should have got a clue as to Paul Dominy's personality by the way he wrote down the requested gear information. It was extremely precise and detailed and written in impeccably neat, tiny writing. The gig duly went well and I wrote a rave review, sealing my good relationship with the band for years to come. Actually approaching the musicians and establishing a connection with them made everything much more satisfying - although this was to become a controversial topic in years to come.

We can now fast-forward several years. Paul and I had become good pals, which was unusual because, despite not being particularly antisocial, I have never been someone with many close friends. Somehow we just hit it off and when we both had small children, our families bonded as well. We even undertook a few semi-disastrous holidays together in places such as Brittany and the Norfolk Broads. As a measure of how close we became, I was instrumental in helping to talk Paul through a subsequent divorce when he visited me in my rented caravan in Dorset to try and get his head together.

Paul was already in a new relationship and living in a tiny terraced house in Southsea when we visited him in 2001, to find him in the midst of a professional crisis. Somehow, he was in the process of being moved from his job with Cendant in Portsmouth and invited to relocate to work for them in Oklahoma. Not surprisingly, this precipitated a dilemma of life-changing proportions, as the family struggled with the prospect of uprooting themselves and relocating to the other side of the world. We eavesdropped on the phone conversation Paul was having with his potential new boss in Tulsa, as they discussed the practicalities.

Fast forward to 2022, when Birgit, younger daughter Lucy and I found ourselves in the searing heat of Tulsa, Oklahoma, visiting the Dominys in their new home there. During the visit, Paul and I went out to a couple of woeful gigs by dire cover bands in local clubs, but we enjoyed the shared experience of live music and discreetly taking the piss out of the hapless musicians. One band, aptly called Uninvited Guest, was definitively the worst act that either of us had ever seen and would forever become a benchmark by which to measure shit bands.

Here, I will go into our friendship in more depth.

I call Paul my best friend and I'm pretty sure that is reciprocated. For the first years of our friendship, life was dominated by band management and subsequently by child management, and it wasn't until we started going to South By Southwest that we began to spend large amounts of time together, just the two of us. Like the basis of many friendships and, of course, marriages, we are completely dissimilar people but we understand each other and know each other inside out. I am quite a boring person from the point of view of character. I don't tend to have great fluctuations in mood or habits, but I am an extremely anxious individual and worry about almost everything almost all of the time.

Paul, on the other hand, has a more confident personality and is definitely better organised, but one thing about him is that, over the years, he has fluctuated in certain of his attitudes. For example, before reaching his current plateau of general middle-aged contentment, when I first started going to Austin he had enthusiastically embraced some of the less advisable American lifestyles, which included eating too much unhealthy food, certainly drinking too much and taking little exercise. In those first two years of SXSW, Paul was happy to cheerfully describe himself as a "fat bastard". Nowadays, the modern-day Paul is embarrassed to look back on those times and shudders if I threaten to produce old photographs.

Looking back, I don't really know why, because it is so far from Paul's progressive attitudes nowadays, but there was a certain 'laddish' element to him as he would slap me on the back, enticing me to have yet another beer when I had had quite enough already, and accusing me of being wimpish when refusing to eat large steaks and greasy burgers. We do have a fine tradition which dates back to many years ago when Paul would claim that he liked nothing better than a "gurt lump of meat". The word 'gurt' has long since entered our vocabulary as being a synonym for a bottle of beer: "Fancy a gurt?" "Don't mind if I do". These dietary habits could cause problems, particularly when Paul would suddenly decide that he had to eat instantly, and disappear into some restaurant in search of sustenance. Oddly, South By Southwest only has limited street food outlets, so often this would mean going through the rigmarole of being shown to a seat, introduced to the server and studying a menu. It could sometimes lead to us missing a couple of bands, which I could find quite upsetting, because my metabolism is such that I can go entire days without feeling hungry.

Another matter altogether, and one which would require an entire chapter of its own, was the effects of the large number of 'gurts' on Paul's bladder, which for some reason would leap into action and demand to be emptied instantly. Toilet facilities outside of restaurants or venues in an American city are non-existent, so Paul would set off at a trot in search of a hotel in which to relieve himself. This led to several interesting discussions, as I would suggest that he should do what I would normally do in such circumstances, which would be to retire behind a bush or down an alley and piss up against the wall. Paul assured me that in American law that would be classified as gross indecency and result in immediate arrest.

One regular destination for bladder emptying was the Holiday Inn hotel in downtown Austin, into which Paul would disappear while I lurked outside feeling embarrassed. One year, inexplicably really, but also oddly satisfyingly, we went into a print shop and had a large sign printed and laminated which we attached to the toilet door in the Holiday Inn. It read 'Welcome to the PJ Dominy Memorial Restroom'. We would pop in to check in the following days and were satisfied to see that the sign remained in situ.

As the South By Southwest years rolled on, Paul flipped to a different extreme and very impressively became a teetotal vegan, and very strict in both of those commitments. Those were the years when I uncharacteristically became the bad boy who drank alcohol and downed greasy pizzas. One huge advantage (to me) of Paul's healthy new lifestyle was that, as a non-drinker, he was able to bring his car to Austin and drive us from gig to gig. This did make me feel mildly guilty, but it was typically generous of Paul. He didn't seem to miss the alcohol at all and it didn't bother him as we buzzed efficiently around from venue to venue.

After a few years of this, Paul decided, quite wisely, to set aside his teetotal vows for one week every March, and now I would say that he has reached an ideal state of equilibrium, whereby he maintains his vegan diet but also isn't averse to a couple of 'gurts' now and then. He is also a super-fit, extremely fast and dedicated cyclist, an activity which he enjoys enormously.

Things such as the Memorial Bathroom and the 'gurts' are small examples of an extraordinarily compatible sense of humour which we share, but which we could not possibly share with anyone else. Based upon a uniquely British in-depth sense of irony, most of our hysterics are based upon saying to each other exactly the opposite of what we actually believe. On matters of politics, society, morals etc, as regards our genuine beliefs, we are fully committed woke pinko lefties, and anything we say that doesn't fit into that kind of philosophy is an elaborate parody of people who do have those attitudes. But we have to be super-careful not to be overheard saying anything seemingly inappropriate, lest anyone should take it seriously. We do have normal conversations too, because we have similar musical tastes and of course both share in the joys of family and grandchildren, about whom we are extremely warm and sentimental and totally of the same mindframe. We also talk about our wives but never complain about them, as we are both privileged to be married to extremely strong and admirable women.

One final thing needed to be sorted. Even on the first SXSW visit, I was on speaking terms with several of the performers. Paul wanted none of this, and came up with the verb 'fawning' to describe my interactions with musicians I knew (mainly from having promoted gigs with them in the UK). What I saw as a pleasant chat was interpreted by Paul as grovelling to people because they were famous, and he found it intensely embarrassing. This was a misunderstanding of what was going on, I felt, particularly as none of my musician friends were remotely famous. Eventually, there was a happy ending, because gradually, Paul came round to appreciating the pleasures of hanging out with genuinely delightful musicians with no motivation other than having a good time with people you like, and fawning is now a word used by both of us as a synonym for 'spending time with'. "Oh look, there's so-and-so ... shall we go over and do a bit of fawning?" "Don't mind if I do". Indeed, Paul now hosts house concerts in his home in Tulsa featuring artists like Will Johnson, Anders Parker and Jenifer Jackson, all of whom he first met at SXSW. You will see from the following reviews that the band that has encapsulated Austin and SXSW for both of us is the late-lamented Centro-Matic, so it is particularly heart-warming that Will Johnson (who is now a vital part of Jason Isbell's band) has played house concerts for both Paul and me, a continent apart. If that doesn't show the merit of 'fawning', I don't know what does.

GEARING UP

Returning to 2003, my relationship with Amplifier magazine was blossoming. With the encouragement of the supportive editor, I was compiling regular reviews, features and interviews for them. They seemed to enjoy the kudos of having their own pet UK correspondent and regularly sent me CDs for assessment. During this time I covered scores of bands with unlikely names such as Pineforest Crunch, The Notwist and Abandoned Pools. Coincidentally, both Paul and I had been reading about the South By Southwest Festival and dreaming of one day attending it. I told Paul all about Austin and the music scene there and we began to make plans for a visit. The UK music magazines would always cover the festival and both of us had been struck by a startling news story entailing a violent incident involving the band Afghan Whigs at SXSW. It all seemed enticingly exciting but of course we realized that we would never be able to afford to attend such an expensive event.

Suddenly, I realized I was potentially sitting on a way in. With no hope at all of success, I contacted Amplifier's editor Joe and asked if he might be able to get me a press credential to attend the festival as a reviewer. It turned out that he indeed could, and he put me in direct contact with someone who would turn out to be extremely important for the future, a lady called Elizabeth who was (and is) head of the press department for the festival.

So what is South By Southwest? I started to do a bit of research on the history of this unique event.

If you tell people you are going to SXSW, they will assume you're at a music festival along the lines of Glastonbury. In fact, it's nothing of the sort. For a start, it takes place indoors, taking advantage of the scores of music venues scattered round the city. It's also based principally around a conference, attended by music business movers and shakers. And most importantly for SXSW as an entity, it isn't only about music but also about film and technology. Each March, over a three-week period, there are three conferences: Interactive, Film, and climaxing with the Music Festival.

The original concept, when SXSW first took place in 1987, was simply to create a music event. This was because Austin was already established as an artistic hub. The group that came up with the idea wanted the city of Austin, the state capital of Texas, with its strongly locally recognised creative streak, to be associated in the wider public mind - worldwide indeed - with music. It wasn't until 1994, when SXSW was well-established, that it expanded into the fields of film and tech.

From reading reviews in UK music magazines, we had a vague idea what SXSW Music would be like. There were seminars, talks and showcases, mainly the sphere of music industry insiders, but all over the city, in the kinds of bars and clubs that Birgit and I had first tasted a few years before, there were gigs, hundreds and hundreds of them. Big bands, little bands, pop bands, rock bands, folk bands, jazz bands, country bands, all kinds of bands, would play their hearts out over the four days of the festival, in the hope of maybe being discovered and promoted to the big time. The days of record company executives with bulging chequebooks in search of the Next Big Thing were pretty much already at an end when we first started attending SXSW, but as any aspiring musician will tell you, hope springs eternal.

This was fertile ground for a music maniac such as myself and before long, Joe from Amplifier had obtained from press officer Elizabeth the promise of the much-coveted 'badge', or press pass that would allow me to attend and review the event. This proved that Amplifier was a credible and respected publication, and I relished getting my teeth into the event.

But what about Paul? How was he to be involved? He was established in a well-paid job in America, but not even that would enable him to afford to pay the full price of a badge, which we knew to be several hundred dollars. Undaunted, Joe enquired whether Paul was a good photographer? I had no idea, but seeing which way the wind was blowing, I replied that he definitely was, and before long, Paul had been assigned the role of official photographer, albeit allocated a slightly inferior wristband, rather than a badge. This swiftly provided much scope for ribaldry as, in order to get into venues, I had to join the queue (or 'line') for Very Important People while Paul had to join a different line for Not Quite So Important People, before rendezvousing inside. There were only a couple of occasions when a place was so rammed that I gained admission and he didn't, but that didn't really cause any difficulty.

Armed with my mission of doing one general review for Amplifier, another for Logo and a Winchester-specific one for the Mid Hants Observer, it was time for the first nervous foray into the madness of SXSW. At this stage, finance reared its ugly head and remained an issue for the following twenty years. Privileged as we were to have free admission to the music, that was only the beginning. First, affordable transatlantic flights for me had to be located, a job that was carried out by trawling a succession of budget flight websites. There was no direct route to Austin, so that first year, a convoluted compilation of connections was worked out, starting in Southampton and stopping over in Amsterdam and Chicago. This had the advantage of starting close to home, but the disadvantage of lasting a total of fourteen hours and involving first a tiny plane (Flybe), then a huge one (Delta) and finally a packed medium-sized one (US internal flight). In subsequent years, similar journeys involved stopovers in Manchester, Minneapolis, Chicago, Newark and Houston, until eventually in 2014, British Airways introduced direct flights to Austin, putting an end to the anxiety-inducing rigmarole of flight connections.

The immigration queue in pretty much any of the American airports was hellish, an endless virtually immobile snake consisting of various queues merging into each other. Inevitably, I always selected the slowest-moving queue and equally inevitably the person in front of me always had issues that would take half an hour to sort out. Invariably, though, the intimidating-looking border officials were actually very friendly and extremely interested in my declared destination of Austin, Texas and my purpose of travel, which was to attend a music festival. "Enjoy", they would say, waving me through to the person who wanted to know if I was importing fruit or meat products.

The cheap flight website had of course planned a connection that was only just attainable and inevitably the connecting flight was only reachable by running down crowded corridors and cramming onto various types of shuttle. On one occasion, the machine that shuttled passengers from one terminal to another was not unlike a gigantic four-wheel-drive tractor. Puffing up to the assembly point for the connecting flight, I realized that it was already full and the fact that I had a ticket was irrelevant. It was my first of many experiences of the extraordinary ritual of staff at the gate offering increasingly higher bribes for people to change from the overbooked flight. It has to be said that this system somehow worked and eventually the bribe was substantial enough for a few people to accept it and free up space for booked passengers such as myself.

On any of these convoluted journeys to Austin, the signs of the Rock And Roll Secret would be apparent from the start, with the transatlantic flights crammed with seedy-looking music biz bods and skinny guys and girls with floppy, dyed black hair, skinny black jeans and leather jackets, the default uniform for any aspiring rock band. Inevitably they have ordered vegan meals that don't turn up and have a dispute with staff over where to place their precious guitars and extremely bulky pedalboards. One time in Manchester, I found myself sitting next to music journalist John Robb with his distinctive Mohican. Another time, in Amsterdam, I was opposite record company owner Simon Raymonde and on numerous occasions I would spot from afar rock stars such as Robert Plant, Chrissie Hynde or various dodgy-looking members of Primal Scream. Anybody remotely rock and roll-looking would tend to get stopped by border officials and given an extra grilling. I once witnessed the luxuriantly-bearded Josh T Pearson being taken into a back room for closer inspection of his voluminous chin furniture. Of course I was far too shy to talk to any of these people and frankly feeling a bit of a fraud anyway, fearful of what I could say if they asked me what I did. One year I ate an entire airline meal that was labelled Rachel Unthank, simply because, although I knew she was sitting two rows in front of me, I was too scared to actually say anything to her.

Having successfully negotiated all the changes, the queues and the fluttering nervous stomach, I would arrive into the grandly-named Austin Bergstrom Airport, and from the moment you landed there you knew that everything from now on was going to be about music. The shops in the airport are branches of venues in town. Some of them actually have singers performing to welcome you as you arrive, and on the luggage carousels, as you wait nervously for your case to appear, you note that the majority of items going round are huge flight cases with stencilled band names on them, containing various keyboards, guitars, amps and drummers' 'breakables', shortly to be collected by the floppy dyed-hair contingent.

One consistent aspect of all journeys to Austin has been that Paul would be waiting for me at the airport, having arrived earlier either by car or by flight from Tulsa and somehow or other we would make our way to our accommodation. Hotels during South By Southwest are the next financial minefield. There are numerous options all over the city, starting with the top level chains such as Marriott or Hilton, which would have been way out of our price range, but, like in any American city, there are hundreds of chain motel-style places whose owners have worked out that every March, there is an influx of festival attendees who need somewhere to sleep and therefore can be fleeced for vastly inflated prices. That first year would set the pattern for years to come, because Paul for some reason had a connection with various chains of hotels via the car rental business that he was working for. This meant that we were able to obtain rooms in a very crowded market, although we still had to pay the inflated price.

The other matter was that these places would be located in far-flung suburbs that were not easy to reach. Downmarket American hotels have certain characteristics that anybody who has ever travelled in the States will recognize. These include outrageously loud and violent air conditioning, two enormous double beds crammed into a small room, a bathroom where the bath never has a plug, and a gigantic TV that you're unlikely ever to switch on. There's also the rather worrying safe which implies that people could potentially gain access to the room in search of valuables, a trouser press that's not much use on a pair of skinny black jeans and a complete lack of anything resembling the most crucial item among any British traveller's requirements: a kettle. True, there is always an incomprehensible coffee machine, but any attempts to make tea in it result in your polystyrene cup containing a murky brown liquid that still smells of coffee.

After the first year, I quickly decided to make a point of bringing a large supply of tea bags from home, because the daily replenished 'hospitality tray' would consist of just one of these items and a little pink sachet of something referred to as 'coffee creamer'. I would always insist that the first stop on the way to the hotel should be at a shop that sold both cold beer and cold milk. After a few years, Paul generously gifted me an electric kettle with an American plug, plus another item always missing from American hotel rooms, namely a hair dryer, or at least a functioning one. This is crucial travel equipment for someone as vain as me, but I regret to say that I have lost both these desirable items. I'm assuming that Paul will one day read this book and this is my confession. I've searched my entire house and all the sheds from top to bottom and I simply can't find them. The excuse I have been giving that I couldn't fit them into my luggage is simply a lie.

Anyway, there is little to choose between any of the American budget hotel chains. Ones we have stayed in over the twenty years have included Super 8, Motel 6 and a selection of Day's Inns, almost all of them positioned on very busy highways with 24-hour uninterrupted traffic noise. A few of them offer some kind of breakfast consisting of over-sweet gooey muffins and plastic plates and cutlery, but my knowledge of the breakfast is minimal, as I could count on the fingers of one hand the amount of times I've actually been up in time to take advantage of them. There's not a lot more to say about hotels really, because my use of them has been limited to staggering into them about 2 am, crashing out till midday and then departing almost immediately.

Every year, prior to locating the accommodation, there is an essential task to undertake, namely picking up 'accreditation' and that vital rectangular piece of plastic on a lanyard that will be around your neck for the next five days. This process takes place in the enormous Convention Center in downtown Austin. I assume that this normally houses slightly more sober conferences but for SXSW every pillar and every square inch of wall space is completely covered with posters, flyers and stickers advertising bands, bands, bands, bands, bands and more bands. You never actually see anybody looking at these items, but there is a definite sense of 'if you can't beat them, join them' as you observe items being sellotaped up, obscuring whatever had previously been there.

In contrast to the mayhem that is the actual festival outside, the Convention Center is a pleasant oasis of quiet. It's calm, air-conditioned and comfortable. In order to obtain your badge, you have to join a long queue and eventually you will reach a cool student who will take a photo of you, press a few buttons and hey presto, the lanyard appears. Then you cross the room to another desk where a little blue plastic label is attached to your camera, allowing you to use it in venues. At least, that was the case back when people actually had cameras. Nowadays everybody in the audience is using their mobile phone throughout the whole of every performance, but the Little Blue Label sometimes gets you into the photo pit for the 'first three numbers no flash' ritual. In the first three years of our attendance, it was crucial for Paul to have the Little Blue Label as he was, if you remember, 'my photographer', but they also gave me one for good measure. This was just as well, because Paul will freely admit that back then, he wasn't a photographer at all and most of my pictures were at least as good as any of his.

Suitably accredited, we would leave the Convention Center staggering under the weight of a tote bag containing a couple of kilos of promotional material. I suspect that being included in this minor treasure trove was something that had to be paid for by the contributors. Among the hundreds of frankly not particularly useful things inside would be numerous CDs, booklets, flyers, posters and pens advertising particular acts and showcases organised by specific countries or companies. For the first few years, we dutifully carried these things back to the hotel and indeed I brought the whole lot all the way back to England on a couple of early occasions, merely to chuck almost everything into the bin at home. I say almost everything, because certain artefacts, if you delved deeply enough into the lucky dip, were actually worth hanging on to: several pairs of branded sunglasses and little plastic pots containing earplugs. In subsequent years, we would have a quick rifle through, grab anything that looked usable and deposit everything else straight into the bin outside the door. Nowadays, in the digital age, all they give you is an empty tote bag, although it must be admitted that the design is always very attractive and the bags, particularly one designed one year by Robyn Hitchcock, have done me sterling service on numerous holidays and camping trips.

The principal and most essential item in the bag was always the official programme and as soon as possible, we would sit down somewhere and start to study it. I will describe the programme booklet because it became an iconic thing in my life and I have a row of them on my bookshelf, which I consult when feeling nostalgic. Sturdy, and presented in a shape and size ideal for insertion into an inside jacket or rear jeans pocket, the booklet listed every official showcase and every band contained within. During that first year, in March 2003, the nerdy but irresistible thing we did was sit down and count the number of bands. It came to 1,243. We also found out that a wristband (not a badge) would have cost us 110 dollars. This induced a certain smugness.

On each page of the booklet were listed all the bands in two formats - by venue and by alphabetical order of artist. Thus, if you wanted to know who was playing at 10pm at the Hole In The Wall on a particular day, you could immediately find out. Alternatively, if you wanted to know when and where you might catch a particular band, you could find that out as well. Also included was a handy little map, making it possible to choose a certain area of town and just plan a jaunt with short walks. But for someone like me, on a mission to catch all the hottest bands of the day and report on them for Amplifier, this was a useless approach and each evening was a logistical nightmare as I attempted, with little help from transport systems, to cover acts that were playing literally miles apart from each other. I say evening, because to our total shame, it took a couple of years for us to realise that shows were taking place at all these venues, plus scores of others, all day, every day, although the booklet only included the 'official showcases'. What exactly that meant, we will come to later, but the showcases only went (and still go) from 7pm to 2am.

With the help of several people I know who have played the festival, I started looking into how it works from the point of view of a performer. The major artists playing big shows get paid the normal kind of fee they would expect, but how is it for the 'tiddlers'? Well, they do get paid, for a start. This is not some kind of 'pay to play' operation. The amount they get paid can vary but it is a reasonable fee for a showcase slot and considering the exposure they get and the infrastructure required for it to take place at all, I think it is fair.

One artist I spoke to explained:

"In 2009 I was offered a fee or a delegate pass, while my manager was also given a delegate pass. So the offer was either two delegate passes, or one delegate pass plus a couple of hundred dollars. We opted for the extra pass, so we could go and see lots of other shows. Bigger (especially headlining) artists get paid substantial fees, as with any festival. They are not 'applying to showcase', it's being booked like a normal festival slot, through their US agent. The payment as a showcaser was both very fair, compared to a normal gig payment for an essentially unknown act, but also minuscule compared to the costs of getting and staying there. I toured small venues across from the west coast and made a decent profit on those shows but still lost thousands of pounds doing South By Southwest. However, the following two years after I played, even though I didn't apply, I got invited back by someone in their organisation, but I couldn't go either time."

For the showcasing artists, there is thus an issue with all the costs associated with getting to Austin and being accommodated there, plus flights for a full band and all their gear. What they get out of it is an exciting adventure and a chance to meet loads of like-minded people, but the likelihood that might have occurred in the olden days of the music industry, that an executive from a major record company might just happen to be the audience, borders on zero.

Many bands playing South By Southwest are simply there for the craic. One example I know is Lee Bains and the Glory Fires. Lee is a hard-rocking Christian radical socialist from Alabama, which is quite something in modern day America, and every year he and his band turn up and charge around in their van with the U-Haul trailer from squalid gig to squalid gig, playing their hearts out to small but wildly enthusiastic audiences. But consider the position of some hopeful from the UK who may, like Winchester's Josh Savage did in 2015, travel all the way there simply to play one sparsely-attended showcase gig. They'll be losing a lot of money but having a lot of fun, so that seems like a result of sorts.

This brings us to the British contingent which pitches up each year and takes over one or other venue for four days to display their wares. For years, it was something called the British Music Embassy at a club called Latitude in the heart of downtown Austin. These are extraordinary events where effectively a ghetto of UK acts play to each other, with virtually no one from the US music scene in attendance. It is cloyingly incestuous, especially with the presence of a huge and highly-subsidised BBC contingent. And talking of subsidies, I dread to think what the average British rate-payer would think of the funding that clearly comes from councils in different regions of the UK to send hopefuls over to America for a jolly-up and an attempt to further their career.

Everywhere you go there are showcases from Japan, Korea, Germany and other far-flung corners of the world. There is definitely some quality control, because applicants have to go through an assessment procedure, while nervously awaiting a decision from the organisers as to whether they have been granted a showcase or not. It would not be in anybody's interest for completely incompetent musicians to show up but believe me, I have witnessed some pretty inept no-hope performances and been sorry to see sincere people wasting their time. Still, like being granted a slot on a far-flung obscure stage at Glastonbury, it must be an enthralling experience that they will never forget. If they can afford it, I guess, why not?

TWENTY YEARS OF SXSW REVIEWS

The review itself is in regular type and
any additional comments added afterwards are in italics.

YEAR 1: 2003 / MARCH 18 - 22

Distilled from reviews in Amplifier, LOGO
and the Mid-Hampshire Observer.

And on the eighth day, God created Austin. If drums and wires rather than milk and honey in the Elysian Fields are your idea of heaven, then South By Southwest is the place for you.

You'll spend your days in a frenzy of charging from venue to venue, stamping with the frustration that the only five bands you want to see are all playing at the same time in different locations. Have you made the right choice? You'll never know. The furthest I had to hike in one go was from Stubbs's Barbecue on Red River to the Continental Club on Congress, a distance of about three miles.

First, the peculiar things. The Joe Jackson band played a storming open-air set to a huge crowd and then another one indoors, just a few hours later. This was surely a flawed managerial decision, and so it proved. The indoor show at the Austin Music Hall was sparsely attended and Joe had lost his voice, cutting short the performance.

This was an odd day to kick off with. In a frenzy of ludicrous over-optimism (it was my first time and my motivations were similar to all those hopeful bands I've just been talking about), I had taken with me a large bundle of flyers advertising my music memoir VOLUME with the intention of handing them out and - hilarious notion - generating sales. As Joe Jackson features in that book, I thought this would be an ideal opportunity. But it was an unusual show for SXSW. Down by the Colorado River there is a wide stretch of land designated as Auditorium Shores, where the public without wristbands can get tickets to one-off shows such as this one. As we waited for Joe to appear (as part of a reunion tour with his original band), I humiliatingly wandered around pressing unwanted flyers into the hands of uncomprehending and uninterested Texans, who promptly dropped them on the ground, causing unnecessary litter. Eventually I was reduced to sellotaping them to the plastic toilet cubicles. Paul, quite rightly, was hugely embarrassed by this and distanced himself from me.

Then, as evening drew in, we planned to experience the indoor JJ show as well, in the nearby cavernous Austin Music Hall. Unversed in the badge etiquette, we were fearful of being unable to gain admission because of overcrowding. There was an obvious solution, I thought, as Paul was well acquainted with Joe's bassist Graham Maby, from Portsmouth band-managing days. Just get Graham to put us on the guest list, I said. But Paul was very reluctant, on account of the aforementioned 'fawning' issue. Paul just didn't like to intrude on the privacy of artists, even if he knew them. It wasn't shyness, as Paul isn't the least bit shy, and it wasn't that he thought Graham would not be pleased to see us or wouldn't be delighted to help us out. He simply found it embarrassing. I, on the other hand, didn't see Graham just as a performer but more of a pal, certainly to Paul. Anyway, I used what powers of persuasion I had and (this being before the availability of text messaging) we agreed to write a note on a piece of paper and hand it in at the stage door. Of course, Graham was happy to oblige and, as it turned out, the place was only half-full (as most people didn't feel our nostalgic need to see Joe Jackson twice) and anyway, he lost his voice and had to abandon the show half way through.

Stranger still was Grandaddy's appearance at a V2 label showcase at La Zona Rosa. They were so woefully under-rehearsed that they struggled through a disastrously disjointed show and were clearly relieved when the stage manager made the cut-off sign. All other bands used this is a signal to do one more number but Granddaddy gratefully scuttled for the exit.

The 'secret' appearance of Blur was fascinating. Alex James had failed to obtain a work permit, so a stand-in bassist was used. What with new guitarist Simon Tong being so understated as to be virtually invisible, this was the Damon show in a big way. Luckily he was up to the job and Blur satisfied everyone with old favourites like Song 2 (introduced as 'Fuck You') and a selection of new songs (all, contrary to rumour, perfectly accessible).

The 'secret show' is a SXSW concept of which we were then unaware, but on every lamp-post round town were posters advertising a bill at La Zona Rosa (another cavernous venue adjacent to the Music Hall), headlined by a 'special guest'. This was also in the programme booklet, one of whose characteristics is to state the geographical origin of each artist. This can give major clues, as in this case: 'Special Guest (Colchester, UK)'. If that wasn't Blur, it would be quite disappointing. Quite clever stuff: Don't tell everyone and face the place being mobbed, but also don't give too few clues and risk the superstars playing to an empty room.

The essence of SXSW is cruising the bars of Sixth Street, sticking your head into each one (ear plugs being a vital necessity) and seeing what gems you can discover. You catch snatches of scores of bands whose names you never find out but some you remember, for diverse reasons. Here is my list: Austin's Andrew Kelly at Mercury (for being quiet), Kinski and Maserati at Emo's (both for being magnificently noisy and sonically ambitious), Spiraling at the Hard Rock Cafe (whose big showcase moment to an empty room was hit by an exploding PA half a song in), Pineforest Crunch at Maggie Mae's for being sweet, Swedish and using a Stylophone, Voyager 1 at Spill for being the only post-Gong space rock band at the entire event, The Features at Spill for being like XTC and for the feeling I one day will boast about seeing them when they were 'small' *(ahem)* and New Jersey's Rye Coalition for being the hardest rocking mothas of very many hard rocking mothas.

That's an interesting list. I must have chosen all those bands because they were the ones I identified as being most likely to survive. Maybe their mention in Amplifier would be their first in a long and glittering career? Sadly, I fear that none of them had any significant kind of breakthrough or even exist any more. The same applies to the venues, of which there is a startlingly high turnover. Maggie Mae's is still there but the others have all either disappeared or been re-named.

Being in Texas, it was vital to catch some country rock. It was odd, then, that the best country came from Canada (Kathleen Edwards), from Australia via the UK (Grand Drive) and from Devon (Peter Bruntnell). Edwards, despite her engaging personality, upfront lyrics and rocking band, gave little real clue as to why she has so suddenly burst forth from a very crowded and competitive market. Of equal interest was a young Austinite called Sarah Sharp, who popped up all over the place. Grand Drive stole the show at a UK Showcase at the Ritz, admittedly not much of an achievement because this over-promoted but under-attended event featured some of the UK's most sludgy and uninteresting rock bands.

I cannot understand why I was so grudging about Kathleen Edwards. In my opinion today, she is the greatest country-rock artist there has ever been and I apologise publicly for expressing those doubts in 2003. As for Sarah Sharp, well, that was the beginning of a friendship that lasts to this day. Sarah had emailed me through some connection to Peter Bruntnell and was hoping for coverage of her new album. There wasn't much I could do in that respect, not being an album reviewer, but what I could do was arrange some UK gigs for Sarah and her Welsh then-husband Andy. As their family expanded, we remained in touch and Sarah has now found her niche as an established jazz singer, entertaining crowds all over Austin on a regular basis.
It was a not dissimilar story with Grand Drive actually. That

show at the Ritz was an incredibly hot and tense affair. I think band dynamics can tend to lead to a lot of tension, which often creates some of the best shows. It's hard to think back to those days when stardom was a serious prospect for Grand Drive and the band seemed completely out of reach to the likes of me. Nowadays Danny is a crucial part of the London live scene and his gregarious and affable personality is familiar to one and all.

Now the bit my editor hates, namely the cool bands that I missed. Excuses include inability to locate the venue, clashing with something possibly inferior and having to eat or else faint. Here's that list of shame: Kaito, Longwave, Raveonettes, Cat Power and Drive By Truckers. Other categories include those where overcrowding meant it was physically impossible to get in (The Coral at Stubb's), ones where I didn't think it would be good but apparently it was (Leona Ness, complete with Peter Buck) and bands I missed on purpose because I disapprove of them (British Sea Power, for abuse of foliage).

A feature of this first review will be repeated throughout all the subsequent ones, and that is the discovery of numerous bands which are described as destined for enormous success, yet strangely are never heard of again. Well, it is part of the job of your journeyman music writer to try and discover the future of rock and roll, and after a few beers it's easy to think that you have identified exactly that. Looking back from the perspective of years later, you realize that, out of at least a thousand bands at each SXSW, although it's possible that you might find the future of rock and roll in one of them, it's actually unlikely. That does not prevent you from being regularly deceived in this way. The opposite also applies frequently, in the form of slagging off someone who is destined for stardom. My best previous effort in that respect was a review of an early Oasis gig in Portsmouth which described them as 'marginally less interesting than a slumbering lugworm'. At the time, I felt it was accurate, but in later years I became quite an Oasis fan. Please feel free to ignore all the 'tips for the top' that you will find in the following pages, because virtually all of them were completely unfounded, unjustified and inaccurate.

In an environment that was often more than a tad self-reverential, some welcome humour came from the Trachtenberg Family Slide Show Players. The excellently geeky dad, accompanied by his young drummer daughter Rachel, are a Moldy Peaches-type novelty act that certainly puts a new perspective on White Stripes, Kills-style duos. Their songs are written around old 35mm slides that they find in flea markets and, as the man from the Austin Chronicle said, "You ain't lived until you've heard a nine-year-old girl demanding 'more vocal in the monitors'".

The rejuvenated Camper Van Beethoven, also at La Zona Rosa, were another high point. Not only was David Lowery one of the surprisingly few people to make a clear, unequivocal and impassioned anti-war speech but they also did a roaring Take The Skinheads Bowling, following up with their unique interpretation of Fleetwood Mac's Tusk and, yes, Status Quo's Pictures of Matchstick Men. And then, in an event overflowing with sound and light freakout grand climaxes, they produced by far the most explosive and entertaining one of all. Phew!

Which brings us to the answer to the inevitable "What was the highlight?" question. Luckily there was no competition. On their home turf, completely selling out the huge Music Hall and then making it impossible to get anywhere near Stubb's, The Polyphonic Spree proved that they are one of the most original, intelligent, charming and just plain brilliant acts in the history of rock music ever. And boy, were they on form. We worked out that you'd have to see them 23 times to fully appreciate them, as each member merits study for the entire performance. Paul's tip: front row, extreme right of the choir. My tip: the theramin player.

That's SXSW then. Hope I'll get my breath back before next year.

DIARY HIGHLIGHTS:

Wednesday 11pm. The Jungle Brothers are supporting And You Will Know Us By The Trail Of Dead at Emo's. This is the sort of mad juxtaposition which makes SXSW so extraordinary. The assembled Texans refused to shake their booty and Trail Of Dead caused no mayhem at all. Emo's is typical of Austin venues, consisting of some outside stages and a couple of inside rooms, all with bands blasting away at unthinkable volume, leaking into each other's sonic territory. This is not a place for purists.

Thursday 9 a.m. I adopt a policy which enables me to obtain my complimentary breakfast and still get some sleep by setting the alarm for 9, grabbing a couple of unpalatable items from the dining room, and then going back to sleep till mid-afternoon. Quite a pleasant lifestyle actually.

There's a young girl who busks outside a bank on Sixth Street every evening. She's so good that she draws a crowd bigger than some of the music bars.

Friday 12:00 am: The Frames are playing on something akin to someone's patio. Their set is completely chaotic, but somehow fitting. You can hear the two bands on either side more clearly than the Frames. Next door, a battered sign offers 'The best fajitas in the USA'. We go back there three times to verify the claim but it's never open.

Saturday 4 pm. We meet Dallas Patterson, who is an unemployed person who does the city a great service by collecting empty beer cans in a shopping trolley and recycling them. We think this is a fine example to us all.

Saturday, 10pm: Just outside the Cactus Café on Guadaloupe, I'm approached by a bruised and battered young man, who asks for a cigarette. His name is Clint and he's spent the whole of South By Southwest in jail on account of a police car chase which he lost on Tuesday night. His dad has had to come up with $10,000 to bail him out.

VENUE SPOTLIGHT: WATERLOO RECORDS

Chapter 2 of this book related my unsuccessful attempt to locate Billy Bragg at Waterloo Records. Waterloo has a long and proud record of putting on in-store concerts by artists who come through Austin to promote their new material, but during South By Southwest the store ups its game dramatically with large-scale shows in their car park. Sometimes, as when putting on popular local band Spoon, the capacity is insufficient and nearby roads are clogged with people trying to listen over the fence. Promoter in chief has been Jessie, the wife of Centro-matic's Will Johnson, who worked at Waterloo Records for a number of years.

Memorable shows there include a typically endearingly shambolic show by Granddaddy and an extraordinary event by A Place To Bury Strangers, who decided to perform in the middle of the crowd with a tiny satellite PA on a trolley. My most memorable visit to Waterloo was in 2023, when I was on a mission to get a press photograph of the Zombies, who were playing a small duo show on the inside stage. Actually pinning them down was quite a difficult task in the cramped conditions but the wait was enlivened by a chat with 60s icon Dana Gillespie, who was in the crowd and under the mistaken impression that Paul and I were influential journalists. Just down the road from Waterloo is a branch of Barnes and Noble and together they form the scene of one of my greatest humiliations. In the year 2012, I decided to write a crime novel that was largely set during SXSW. It was called Zander and I was hoping that the good folk of Austin would be captivated by it and wish to buy it in local shops. I had communicated by email with both Waterloo and Barnes & Noble and assumed that they might be expecting me, but on arrival clearly nobody had any idea what I was talking about and neither venue displayed the slightest interest in the book. They didn't even want to accept free copies, which they could potentially have sold and kept the profit, so I was reduced to secretly placing a few copies on their shelves, something I also did at the Yard Dog Gallery on South Congress. For all I know, the books are still there. I have learnt my lesson and certainly won't be placing any copies of this one there.

BANDS SEEN IN 2003

And You Will Know Us By The Trail Of Dead
Blur
Peter Bruntnell
Camper van Beethoven
Kathleen Edwards
The Features
Guy Forsyth
The Frames
Grand Drive
Grandaddy
The Joe Jackson Band
The Jungle Brothers
Kinski
Sonny Landreth
Maserati
Pineforest Crunch
The Polyphonic Spree
Rye Coalition
Bob Schneider
The Thrills
The Trachtenberg Family Slideshow Players
Voyager 1

YEAR 2: 2004 / MARCH 16 - 20

Distilled from reviews in Amplifier, LOGO
and the Mid-Hampshire Observer.

Here's a taste of the uniquely enjoyable madness that is South By
Southwest. Every evening, all evening at the junction of Sixth and
Trinity, a group of Christian evangelists try to convert the many
thousands of sinners streaming past. As every building is shaking to
the bone-shattering volume of punk bands, rock bands, metal bands,
blues bands and Japanese hardcore glam-slam bands, the only way
they can convey their message is to shout. But they are not alone.
Permanently challenging them is a wizened old hippie dressed in
nothing but a skimpy leopardskin chemise and a thong. His method
of countering God's word is to shout even louder than them. He
roars terrifyingly into their faces for as long as they are there, which
is a long time. It's great entertainment but there's no time to spare,
for we have 1200 bands to see.

The madness continues. In an event where eccentricity is almost
de rigeur, Robyn Hitchcock comes across as being perfectly normal.
London singer Paul The Girl, dressed in a silver lamé dress and a
trilby, is playing a looped Led Zeppelin song to fifteen people on the
eighteenth floor of the Hilton Garden Hotel. They are warming up - I
kid you not - for Jamie Cullum.

At Elysium, the singer of one of the many Japanese all-girl groups
present is reading her between-song patter from cue cards. The front
row of the audience is having a great time. "Say 'rock and roll'",
they plead.

South By Southwest is famously impossible to review because at any one moment, scores of bands are playing concurrently in different places. Teeth-grinding dilemmas are a permanent reality. Franz Ferdinand or Athlete? Razorlight, The Veils or The Gourds? How do you decide? Why, you drink loads of beer and do whatever seems right at the time. My best example: Choosing Drive By Truckers rather than the Polyphonic Spree, on the basis that it would be easier to get in.

So what is the 'real' SXSW? Is it the industry bashes, where labels and national cultural agencies show off their new artists? These ones are good to suss out because they sometimes dole out free beer. The UK Showcase 'pre-party' (I may have the terminology wrong) saw snooty music journalists mingling with BBC Radio 2 DJs and the likes of Tom MacRae and Thea Gilmore being terrifyingly cool. Refreshingly uncool and simply charming were Aqualung, who played this event acoustically. "We've never played at a wedding before", observed Matt Hales, who incidentally hails (sorry) from Winchester. He was referring to the starched white tablecloths.

I had been tasked with handing out free copies of Amplifier magazine at the festival, in order to raise awareness among the music biz establishment, so I chose this schmoozefest as the ideal opportunity. As several of my articles were in the latest edition, I felt a tingle of mild pride as I pressed copies into the hands of influencers such as Paul du Noyer of Q magazine and Stuart Maconie of BBC Radio One, only to observe both of them casually depositing them, unread, into the bin. (And yes, since you ask, I did retrieve them.)

Nearer to the 'real' SXSW was the brunch party at Maria's Taco Express hosted by Alejandro Escovedo, a respected Austin musician who was currently much in the limelight on account of a serious illness. As breakfast burritos crunched all around, the huge but cuddly Nicholas Tremulis pricked the bubble refreshingly with some swampy Chicago Blues. "If there's anyone influential out there", he cried with unusual candour, "don't sign us, we suck".

Even closer to the 'real' South By Southwest, maybe on account of being miles from anywhere and conducted in the Church Of The Friendly Ghost, a prefab on a suburban trailer park, was the Ba Da Bing party, featuring Sons And Daughters, a Glasgow band who are relishing the increasing attention their entertaining mutant punk-folk is receiving. They have the added advantage of being friends with Franz Ferdinand, which means that they are going to be heard by lots of people *(ahem)*. Seldom has a band been more drunk.

Ah, Franz Ferdinand! The event in which an act that no one has heard of is booked into a little venue but then turns out to be the hottest ticket in town is definitely part of the real SXSW. The mayhem of this show is hard to describe and there is absolutely no doubt that FF is a great band, but there is a certain arch knowingness about them that takes the edge off. Credit where it's due, but once you've got it into your head that Alex Kapranos is actually Wilko Johnson and Nick McCarthy is a member of Spandau Ballet, it's hard to concentrate. Whatever you do, don't try to stare out the bassist. He's scary. So allow me to observe that the band immediately before FF, namely Clearlake, stole the show as far as I was concerned. With their pastoral melodies, melancholy lyrics and unstudied low-key delivery, this is a band whose patience will one day be rewarded *(ahem)*.

If you can get over the feeling of "Oh god, what if there's a fire?", Stubb's Bar-B-Q on Red River is probably the best place to be. Here I contrived to see Detroit's Von Bondies twice by mistake. Las Vegas semi-new romantic revivalists The Killers impressed too, as did the showbiz-dedicated Hives, trying out some new songs on us.

One really rewarding thing to do at SXSW is go and see a band that you liked before and find that they don't let you down. Stellastarr* opted to play a little show at the Red Eyed Fly rather than a schmoozy showcase, and it worked. This is a band you should take someone to see who wants to understand what rock and roll is all about. They are just incendiary *(ahem)*. Similarly undisappointing was Jesse Malin at the Cedar Street Courtyard. This New York ex-punk is charming, literate and humorous, plus has a lovely voice and great songs.

Mentioned in dispatches: Sarah Sharp, whose do-it -yourself ethic has resulted in Fourth Person, an accomplished album that should kick-start her career; International Noise Conspiracy, deft masters of scissor-kicking, microphone-lassooing and vying with the Hives in the Scandinavians In Daft Outfits stakes; Robyn Hitchcock (it's true he's still big in the States); The Black Keys, whose turn-it-up-to 11 distorted blues couldn't have found a more appropriate home than Antone's; American Music Club, who gave the lie to the notion that legends shouldn't reform; and, representing the huge Aussie contingent, a shockingly well-behaved Sleepy Jackson. After two technical breakdowns, even the mildest-mannered band would have smashed up their instruments but the Sleepys' mood was positively mellow. Disappointments: the Veils (it just doesn't work); Graham Parker (he's been doing the same thing for too long); Electrelane (amateurism can sometimes be good but not in this case) and Cerys Matthews (who looked and sounded virtually unrecognizable in her perfunctory set). If this all seems a bit indie for you, it's worth mentioning that other artists appearing included NERD, Kris Kristofferson and, oh yes, Joan Jett and the Blackhearts.

No two reviews of SXSW will mention the same bands and certainly none will agree on a highlight. Mine had the unexpected bonus of being a bolt out of the blue. The scruffy, unkempt bunch of apparent Austin slackers called Centro-matic didn't look promising at all, but the explosive performance of their anthemic songs (think Radiohead meets Neil Young with a healthy dollop of grunge thrown in) caught the soporific audience on the hop, chewed them up and spat them out, exhausted. It was a low-key afternoon affair at The Red Eyed Fly so there probably weren't any A & R men shouting "sign 'em", but there certainly should have been.

LEXICON OF USEFUL GENERIC STAGE PATTER FOR BANDS SHOWCASING AT SXSW:

"Check check check check check."
"More acoustic in the wedge."
"Are y'all having a great South By?"

"We gotta new record coming out on the xxx label."
"Here's a new song."
"You may know this one."
"This one's a cover."
"Have we got time for three more?"
"We gotta couple more for ya."
"We got just one more for ya."
"You guys have been awesome."
"Come and see us at the merch table."

PARANOID ANDROID

So there we were, two years in and already determined to return every year. But how could we ensure that? It was vital to remain in the 'good books' of the organisers, and in our case, this meant always doing our best to produce coverage that would meet with the approval of our friend Elizabeth in the press office, in whose hands rested our fate. I was forever fretting about whether my publications would be deemed not influential or widely-enough read to merit the complimentary media badge, without which attendance would be impossible. Because the event was so brilliant, it was in my mind vital for me to come up with as much good quality coverage as possible. Therefore, many conversations between Paul and me would revolve around the topic, "What will Elizabeth think?"

I started to worry that my reviews were featuring too many 'unofficial' shows, because we had belatedly realised that these went on all day, every day and mainly duplicated showcases in the official programme. How would the organisers react if I wrote about those events rather than their official ones? We therefore resolved to attend as many Official Showcases as possible and make sure they were covered. In reality, this was probably vastly over-thought. We had no real reason to think they would even notice or care, but that's the nature of paranoia.

It felt important to demonstrate to the press office that I was indeed worth the free badge. After each festival, you receive, as a media person, instructions to prove that you have covered the event as promised. In early years, this meant that I would actually cut out the physical paper articles and post them to Elizabeth. Then, as scanning and emailing became more the norm, it would be a matter of copying the paper items and sending them to the press office online. In the lean years, where the papers I was writing for were local ones in the UK, it helped that the pages were in colour and highly-illustrated. Also helpful was that each year there would be various hopeful artists from the Hampshire area trying their luck in Texas. I made a point of attending their shows and writing copiously about them, in order to maximise the likelihood of the coverage getting printed. Performers in this category included, over the years, Josh Savage, Jerry Williams, Flyte, Andy Burrows, Band Of Skulls, Dlugokecki, Chris T-T, Frank Turner, Rozi Plain and Kate Stables (both later of This Is The Kit).

Nowadays it is less clear that badges are available for small-time writers, because so little appears in newsprint. Anyone can create their own blog and can claim to be a journalist even if they only have twenty readers, so presumably the press office must now have very stringent criteria.

I never use my own blog for a SXSW review but luckily, I still have two quite credible websites to write for, plus the print outlet of Record Collector. I fancifully believe that Paul and I continue to be awarded our badges as a kind of recognition of long and dedicated service, but I know of a contingent of Brits who go to Austin each March without a badge or even a wristband. They claim that they have just as good a time, but that can't actually be true. They don't get access to the nightly showcases, to big shows at places like Stubb's or the Moody Theater, or the facilities at the Convention Center. This certainly must limit the experience.

One particularly rewarding aspect of SXSW is the opportunity to experience favourite bands several times. This isn't normally offered at a conventional gig or festival, where that feeling you get, having enjoyed a particularly intense performance, that you'd like to experience it again, isn't normally possible to indulge. You might have to wait years to see the act again, or never see it again, or have to go to some huge stadium to see it again, whereas at SXSW, all you need to do is work out where their U-Haul van is heading, and follow it. Paul and I have occasionally taken this to extremes, though. You'll see from the ensuing chapters that we have been prone to identifying exciting acts and chasing them obsessively. Examples of this phenomenon are Mark Mallman, Centro-Matic, Lee Bains and the Glory Fires and, most prominently, Chuck Prophet and the Mission Express. This band is so ridiculously brilliant that they have to be experienced as often as humanly possible, until you know the entire set by heart, yet still find it intensely stimulating. This is by way of an apology for the vast number of references to Chuck and his band in these pages, and an explanation of the extreme upset induced when it temporarily seemed, in 2022, as if Chuck's illness was possibly going to curtail the band's activities.

I'm sensitive about my age and very aware that I get stared at for being so very clearly one of the oldest people in attendance at SXSW. Mike Trotman, a UK promoter from Oxford, attends each year and has me hands-down beaten in the geriatric stakes, being well over eighty. I've caught people nudging each other and pointing at me and my wrinkles, clearly wondering what a pensioner is doing intruding on their youthful territory, but that's just ageism and unfair. The funniest thing is being stopped and asked for ID to gain admission to almost any venue. My libertarian side wants to refuse to hand my personal details to any random door person who demands them, but if you refuse, you won't get in, simple as that. After a few beers, I will always say, "Just look at me, do you really suspect that I may not be 21?", but it never cuts any ice. These guys epitomise the term 'jobsworth' and won't even respond with a smile.

The laminate round your neck also presents problems if you, like me, are over-sensitive. People feel they have licence to approach well into your personal space in order to examine what it says, before greeting you by your first name, as if you are a long-lost friend. The designation on the card awakens curiosity. For the first few years, it was Amplifier, which invited conversations about amplification. Then it was the Hampshire Chronicle: "Oh, you're from New Hampshire?" Currently it says Record Collector, which always invites, "Oh, you're a record collector? So am I". A high percentage of the conversations dwindle rapidly when your interlocuter realises that, whoever you are, you are unlikely to be able to further their career, so they move on to examining someone else's laminate instead.

We owe it all to Elizabeth in the Press Office and guess what, in the entire 20 years, I have only ever met her once (for a brief thirty seconds) and Paul has never met her at all. Before we are finally too decrepit to attend, we are determined to find Elizabeth, buy her a drink and get our photo taken with her, just to prove she exists (and to say thank you).

BANDS SEEN IN 2004

American Music Club
Aqualung
Athlete
The Black Keys
Centro-Matic
Clearlake
Drive-By Truckers
Alejandro Escovedo
Franz Ferdinand
Thea Gilmore
The Gourds
Robyn Hitchcock
The Hives
The Killers
Jesse Malin
Cerys Matthews
Tom McRae

Paul The Girl
The Polyphonic Spree
Razorlight
The Sleepy Jackson
Sons And Daughters
Stellastarr*
Nicolas Tremulis
The Veils
Ben Weaver

YEAR 3: 2005 / MARCH 15 - 19

Distilled from reviews in Amplifier, LOGO
and the Mid-Hampshire Observer.

I'm having a disturbed night in the motel. Is it traffic? Is it someone having an argument or noisy sex? Is it indigestion from the 10 beers and the burger that I consumed at 4 am? No. This being South By Southwest, the disturbance turns out to be my next door neighbour spending the small hours of the night loudly practising his vocal scales. I refrain from banging on the wall and insert the ever-useful earplugs found in the bottom of my tote bag.

South By Southwest 2005 started out unaccountably freezing. As I shivered on Wednesday evening at Stubb's, I wondered whether the festival had peaked too soon, since the very first band on stage was so fantastic. The heavenly Hammond organ of Detroit's The Sights was like a 2005 take on The Nice. After guitarist Eddie Baronak had destroyed his own instrument, he disembowelled the Hammond for good measure. Judging by the horror on the face of its owner, Bobby Emmett, this was not rehearsed.

On to the Vibe, where, with the acknowledgement that SXSW is a unique and brilliant experience, I must do the unthinkable and criticise something.

The Vibe, as it was called then, is a venue in 6th Street that has changed its name almost every year. It kind of deserves a Venue Focus of its own but I don't want to give it any extra publicity. Of all the many rundown and seedy venues in Austin, this provided the worst imaginable experience. The odd thing about it was that the event was promoted by the cool UK magazine Uncut and had a very strong alt-country / Americana line-up. It was set up to be one of the highlights of the week. How wrong could you be? The stage was rickety, the sound equipment appalling, the room itself filthy, but the worst thing was the so-called bathroom, where there were no hand washing facilities and the urinal had been ripped off the wall and was dangling in mid-air. None of this prevented the male clients from continuing to piss in it, which created an inch deep flood of urine all over the floor. I dread to think what the female facilities must have been like. The sound crew was simply incompetent but, worse than that, they didn't care and spent most of the time away from the sound desk, smoking and chatting. The artists did their best to somehow put on some kind of a show. Poor Deborah Kelly of the Damnations had come specially in order to sing one verse on Richmond Fontaine's Post To Wire, but her microphone was not switched on, so not one note could be heard. South San Gabriel and Willard Grant Conspiracy struggled through brief sets before scuttling away. Mark Eitzel was so enraged by being unable to hear himself on stage that he decided that the audience shouldn't be asked to pay. To emphasise the point, he took his wallet out of his pocket and threw it deep into the crowd. Unexpectedly, the audience meekly returned it to him, passing it, crowd-surfing-like, over their heads back to the stage. At this point, Eitzel threw down his guitar and marched off into the sunset. Meanwhile, I was accompanying Sarah Sharp. She had her debut album out and was keen to speak to anybody who might be influential, so when I spotted Mark Morriss of the Bluetones across the room and pointed him out, she rushed over and engaged him in animated conversation. The baffled look on his face told us that he wasn't quite prepared for this.

Back to the main plot. This year there was an even greater than usual emphasis on bands rushing around to play several showcases in a single day. Thus the super and destined-to-be-huge *(ahem)*

Ambulance Ltd managed only three songs in an afternoon monsoon before having to zoom off for their packed show at Exodus. Other bands 'doing the rounds' included the ubiquitous Duke Spirit, who did themselves proud playing tunes that are likely to appeal to American audiences. Their show at Nuno's was hilarious in that the stage was wobbling enough to induce motion sickness. Meanwhile, the Kaiser Chiefs made a good fist of their battle with Bloc Party for coolest new band but almost suffocated from the weight of the BBC Radio 1 DJs grovelling round them. As he hobbled around on his walking stick with his rosy cheeks and striped blazer, Chiefs' singer Ricky Wilson had the air of a country squire.

Upstairs at Buffalo Billiards (yes, a billiards hall) was the venue for some sensational showcases in the early 2000s. But, not being designed for the crowds invading it as a music venue, it had insufficient toilet facilities. Ricky Wilson, who had sprained his ankle, was hobbling around looking increasingly worried as his stage time approached, because there wasn't anywhere to pee. The ladies' loo being slightly less overcrowded than the gents', he disappeared inside it, jumping the queue by explaining his predicament. Having had a few beers, I simply followed him in, pretending to be part of his crew. Thus it was that Ricky Wilson and I shared a pee in the ladies' bathroom at Buffalo Billiards.

Dogs Die In Hot Cars were a lowlight of the mainly unexciting 'British Invasion'. The band simply does not have what it takes and their unimaginative and derivative set contrasted tellingly with last year's equivalent, the career-launching show from Franz Ferdinand. Other disappointments included Soundtrack Of Our Lives, proving that you need a lot more than posing to ignite an audience, and a much-anticipated performance from Aimee Mann, which turned out to be both turgid and boring.

There were more than enough really great things to counter the disappointments. With a starstruck Bloc Party looking on, the near-perfect Ash were on fire, although drummer Rick McMurray wasn't quite comfortable handling their St Patrick's Day rendition of Thin Lizzy's The Boys Are Back In Town. The unlikely triumph of an incendiary Wreckless Eric at Elysium was a joy to experience. After all, who else would serenade a Texan audience with a song called The Golden Hour Of Harry Secombe? Nashville's Legendary Shack*shakers at the Austin Music Hall were a complete revelation, hurling themselves into their rockabilly circus with total abandon. "Jesus, we're opening for Robert Plant, of course we had to go for it", explained Colonel JD Wilkes after the show. Plant himself predictably brought the house down as the audience communally pinched itself at hearing Whole Lotta Love in all its glory.

Over the years, I suffered quite a few embarrassments caused by unsuccessful attempted 'fawning'. After Wreckless Eric's solo show at Elysium, I felt confident in approaching him for a chat, because it was mere weeks since he had played for us in Winchester, so I was sure he would remember me. I now understand that an artist gets psyched up for a show, putting their all into an intense and sweat-soaked performance, and being cheerfully approached as soon as they get off stage isn't at all appropriate. Eric's reaction to me wasn't negative, just indifferent, but worse was to follow. In his online blog, he launched into a tirade against slimy business creeps with their laminates who pollute the purity of the festival. As I had been sporting my laminate, I was certain he must be referring to me. It wasn't until years later that Eric told me he hadn't meant me at all and hadn't even noticed my laminate. I had been mortified for no reason.

Robyn Hitchcock can always be identified from afar because of his tall stature and famously loud shirts. I spotted him at Stubb's one night, surrounded by admirers, and decided to join in. It was mere days since I had hosted a memorably eventful show by him and the Soft Boys in Winchester, which involved us spending most of a day together, so I was confident that he'd be pleased to see me. In fact, he completely blanked me, turning away from my proffered handshake and carrying on his conversation with his friends. Again, I had behaved completely inappropriately, busting in on him catching up with a bunch of pals in a private context. Nonetheless, my over-sensitivity convinced me he hated my guts. Like with Eric, it wasn't until years later that I mentioned it again (having had numerous entirely civil dealings with him since). He professed to have no memory of the occasion at all. Why should he?

Other fine performances included the ever-brilliant Richmond Fontaine, the charmingly natural and always engaging Embrace, Willy Mason, who was seemingly on every street corner, the over-the-top but fun The Bravery, and an absolute stunner of a show from those uniquely edgy, sexy Kills. Alison Mosshart was certainly the only performer to sing in a full-length overcoat. Those we missed: Billy Idol and Vanilla Ice.

Many mysteries remain to be solved around SXSW. Why are there so many bands from Japan, Australia and Scandinavia yet hardly any from France or Spain? Why do the big venues like La Zona Rosa and Stubb's have admission systems which leave half the audience outside while inside, the venue is often far from full? This, dear reader, is why you will find here no reviews of the New York Dolls, Doves and Futureheads. It wasn't that we didn't try. And finally, why do bands always waste time by unnecessarily swapping guitars between each song (or is this just a bee in my personal bonnet?) *(I didn't realise at the time that it saves previous seconds that would otherwise be used for tuning up.)*

Yes, I know everybody is asking, "Who was the best?" Well, for me there was no competition. For the second year running, the best, most exciting, most musical, most emotionally real and unpolluted band was Centro-Matic from just down the road in Denton, Texas. Forget their unstudied image (a wonderful contrast to many of the bands) and lose yourself in their beautiful, challenging, tough-as-nails music. Their music is at the heart of SXSW and they embody its excellence.

VENUE SPOTLIGHT: RADIO DAY STAGE

There is one SXSW venue where you can see tomorrow's top stars in conditions of great comfort. For some reason, it seems largely unnoticed by many of the festival attendees, possibly because shows tend to take place during the morning and you need a badge to attend. In the Convention Center is a large conference room that gets converted into a theatre, with comfortable plushy seats, a nice carpet and good sound. It calls itself the Radio Day Stage and is an ideal place to catch early performances by tips-for-the-top. Acts I have enjoyed at the Day Stage include Alabama Shakes, Laura Marling, Jake Bugg and Michael Kiwunaka, the last two both performing their first-ever US shows, plus, more recently, great cameos from Wet Leg and Yard Act. The performances tend to be more restrained than regular showcases on account of the refined atmosphere. Afterwards you can nip across the road to Brush Park, where there are free beers for delegates, plus occasional impromptu performances such as that by Amy Winehouse in 2007.

BANDS SEEN IN 2005

Ambulance Ltd
Ash
Bloc Party
The Bravery
Centro-matic
Dogs Die In Hot Cars
Duke Spirit
Embrace
Kaiser Chiefs
The Kills
Th' Legendary Shack*Shakers
Willy Mason

Robert Plant
Richmond Fontaine
The Sights
South San Gabriel
Willard Grant Conspiracy
Wreckless Eric

YEAR 4: 2006 / MARCH 14 - 18

Four things had changed since the previous year regarding my status as a journalist. Amplifier Magazine had followed the fate of most music magazines and gone bust. It had actually gone bust in quite a spectacular way, with editor Joe being accused online of operating a 'pay to play' policy involving asking bands for a financial contribution in return for favourable reviews. I genuinely have no idea about the veracity of this claim, but I can say that I was never asked to do anything like that and never experienced any editorial interference. But as we know, I wasn't getting paid anyway. I was sad to see the magazine go, as I had quite a strong affection for it. At the same time, 'porn-gate' had occurred in Southampton and LOGO magazine had also gone down the pan. Would this twin disaster spell the end of my free badge, effectively meaning the end of my ability to attend SXSW? Miraculously, two things happened that saved the day.

Firstly, my old journalistic alma mater, The Hampshire Chronicle, had started a new 'Arts' section called 'Seven Days', and it included a music page called, with spooky similarity to my recently-deceased outlet, 'Amplified'. I doubted whether Elizabeth would be impressed by the very local nature of the coverage, but as long as there were Hampshire artists playing the festival (and there always were some),

I could be sure of getting a good chunk of newspaper space, with room for some colour photos too.

More significantly, I had become a regular contributor of live reviews to a UK music magazine called Record Collector. This had actually started a couple of years before, but for some reason I'd never thought of submitting anything about SXSW. As far as the SXSW press office was concerned, this was sufficient to replace the two departed glossies, because Record Collector is a legendary magazine. As the oldest of the UK music monthlies, it has survived all the storms that took down rivals such as Q, Select and Vox, the monthlies that replaced the inky weeklies. It has a much higher circulation than any of my other outlets and most importantly, is a national publication. The reviews editor, Tim Jones, sent Elizabeth a letter vouching for my credentials as a contributor and that did the trick. In truth, the Live Reviews section in RC consists of a large number of very brief paragraphs, many of them contributed by readers sending them in. In other words, few of them are commissioned from professional journalists and pretty much anyone who can write reasonably has a strong chance of getting their words printed. Plus, naturally, it is unlikely that any payment will be involved. Of course not! But I have always loved RC, and still do. It's been my passport to free gig admission for two decades and I'm proud to have had hundreds of reviews published by them, including fifteen years of SXSW. It's become quite a tradition.

Distilled from reviews in the Mid-Hampshire Observer, Hampshire Chronicle and Record Collector.

As the BBC has clasped SXSW to its bosom, the UK contingent (punters and bands) has soared. This year it meant an excess of well-spoken, floppy-fringed young men in the post-Keane and sub-Franz Ferdinand categories. My, have those bands got something to answer for. Luckily there were also several less-refined and more entertaining acts around such as The Heights, who pluckily performed two sets when the Editors' gear was rained upon and rendered unusable. The second set was blasted out in a state of hospitality-induced wastedness, and all the more entertaining for it.

In a similar category were the Arctic Monkeys. Great fun, but don't believe the PR. In years to come, marketing students will write dissertations about how this band was promoted. Their show was far from sold out. We walked straight into the venue and to the front of the stage just minutes before they went on; by contrast, the previous night people had queued for hours to get into Morrissey's show. The following day's press reports talked of people clamouring for admission and the Arctic Monkeys being mobbed by teenage girls. Neither claim was true. Anyway, the performance was okay but sloppy, their attempt at gear trashing was feeble and their treatment of the photographers was a disgrace. They love being photographed, they need to be photographed, so to wait until the photo pit was cleared after three numbers and then abuse the snappers as they left was pure hypocrisy. *(A classic and sadly, all too frequent example of my flair for failing to predict success for future megastars.)*

Others who flew the UK flag were mainly bands who wore their influences on their sleeves, respectively the self-same Editors (Joy Division), the bug-eyed, disturbingly manic but strangely entertaining Rakes (Wire) and of course the Mystery Jets (er ... Yes?). At last, a real meaning for Dad Rock. *(This band featured the father of one of the members in the line-up.)*

Old stagers coming up with the goods included The Pretenders, being themselves but with the drummer even more barking than usual (they did an eight song encore, slightly uncalled for as it was pouring with rain) and the highly sought-after Susanna Hoffs and Matthew Sweet (thrilling even observed from behind, as they played in a shop window facing inwards, and incidentally a gig that you wouldn't have got into even if you had waited days). It is little known what turmoil has afflicted World Party in recent years (Karl Wallinger has had brain surgery) but they have been reborn against all the odds and now heavily feature the Blockheads' John Turnbull. The singalong to Put The Message In The Box could have been heard in neighbouring states. Billy Bragg had the tiny Cedar

Street Courtyard hanging on his every word, delving deep into his back catalogue with Greetings To The New Brunette and Milkman of Human Kindness. He also treated the audience to a few well-received home truths about the US administration. How lovely, too, to see the rapturous reception offered to a great act from Iran called 127. Austin isn't at all like certain other parts of Texas. (It can't be emphasised enough that Austin isn't remotely like any clichéd image of Texas, being liberal, tolerant, culturally sophisticated and generally fun-loving).

Keeping an eye out for the legend 'special guests', which normally means something very special indeed, induced optimism as I joined a queue for the Dirty Pretty Things in a little venue called Eternal. Sure enough, after a severe frisking (no cameras allowed), the optimism was justified because there on the little stage were the Flaming Lips setting up their gear. Complete with their giant balloons, confetti and other paraphernalia, they started with their full-length note-perfect rendition of Bohemian Rhapsody and went upwards from there. The community singing on Yoshimi Versus The Pink Robots was heart-warming in the extreme. The hapless Dirty Pretty Things couldn't begin to follow that, sounding like a tenth-rate version of Razorlight and being pulled off after four songs.

Every day at SXSW you meet new people and the first question is always, "What's the best thing you've seen?" No hesitation. If you go straight from a Flaming Lips show and the next performance is even better, it must be really something. Minnesota's Mark Mallman simply destroyed Exodus with the most spectacular, crazy and enthralling stage show you're ever likely to encounter. He's Mr Serious and he's the tops.

I first came across Mark Mallman when he played at the Railway in Winchester, opening for Chuck Prophet and the Mission Express. As he was billed as a solo artist, I was fully expecting the traditional mild-mannered troubadour with an acoustic guitar, but the audience and I were completely flattened when Mark turned out to be spectacularly entertaining, spending much of the time standing atop his rickety electric piano and screaming out his infectiously melodic songs between the strands of his long curly hair. When asked to describe him, the best I could come up with was a cross beween Elton John and Alice Cooper. Thus it was that I made a beeline for each of his performances at South By Southwest, each one more thrilling than the previous, and on one occasion featuring a John Otway-style step-ladder which he ascended to issue his preaching declamations. Mark had made a gorgeous album called Mr Serious, packed with track after track of melodic beauty. I immediately fell into the trap that I have so often before, and occasionally since, caused by feelings of injustice that such an amazing artist could command such a small audience. I felt certain that I could gain interest from the industry for this record in Europe and help set him on the path to international recognition. Mark agreed to send me a large parcel of Mr Serious CDs and I sat down to put together what I thought was an irresistible press release in order to gain maximum coverage from the press and attract potential record companies. Of course, I should have known that the whole thing was completely doomed, because I didn't have the right contacts and no knowledge of how the industry actually works. The fifty or so CDs that I sent out elicited not one single review and not one single response from a record company. I still think that they were all wrong, and dear Mark continues with an intermittently successful career based in his hometown of Minneapolis. I feel strangely sad that not only could I not help him but am also unlikely to get a chance to see him in action again.

VENUE SPOTLIGHT: HEADHUNTERS

Headhunters is one of the few Austin venues that survived for the entire 20 years of this book. Under normal circumstances I don't think we would have even dared enter it, as it looks, from the outside, quite a scary place, certainly with a heavy metal emphasis. But by a series of coincidences we had got to know a Toronto record label called Six Shooter, whose unforgettable strap line was 'Life Is Too Short To Listen To Shitty music', a slogan that Paul identified with so strongly that he had it tattooed between his shoulder blades. As if to prove the point, even in its early days the label had an eclectic line-up of fantastic artists including Luke Doucet, Elliott Brood and the superb (but long since retired from music) slide guitarist Rachelle van Zanten. We received an invitation to their daytime Hootenanny showcase and duly presented ourselves at Headhunters, an absolutely classic SXSW dive. You had to negotiate several dark and pokey rooms, each populated by deafening metal bands, before you reached the space where the showcase took place. There was no stage and hardly any room for an audience. You could either stand directly face-to-face with the artists or risk ascending the rickety staircase and peering over the wooden balustrade, being careful not to actually lean on it for fear of tumbling onto the performers' heads. I've lost count of the number of amazing performances we've seen at Six Shooter showcases, but names that spring to mind include such eccentric Canadian acts as Hot Panda and The Leather Uppers. The entire audience and pretty much all the acts were high as kites on account of the generous portions of tequila being dispensed by label officials including the director Shauna De Cartier, her co-conspirator Helen Britton and assistant Karen Douglas, who was in charge of handing out the free tacos and selling the badges and T-shirts. These unforgettable events summed up the spirit of South By Southwest for me, with an intense feeling of comradeship, companionship and friendship, all wrapped up in brilliant music. After a few years, the label gradually expanded and needed bigger rooms. Eventually they tended to rent an entire house and invite people around for margaritas and extremely potent (so Paul tells me) hashcakes, but for me, those magical Headhunters events will never be forgotten.

Headhunters closed in November 2024 after being featured on the TV show 'Bar Rescue' and the owners got divorced. In 2024, the venue at 720 Red River Street had been repainted and was available for sale or lease.

BANDS SEEN IN 2006

Amazing Pilots
The Arctic Monkeys
Karl Blau
Billy Bragg
The Charlatans
Steve Dawson
Dirty Pretty Things
The Editors
Field Music
The Flaming Lips
The Heights
Susannah Hoffs & Matthew Sweet
Keane
Mark Mallman
Mystery Jets
The Pretenders
Laura Veirs
World Party

YEAR 5: 2007 / MARCH 13 - 17

Distilled from reviews in the Hampshire Chronicle
and Record Collector.

The big names were largely absent from this year's South By
Southwest, which made for a lower-key event that somehow felt
closer to its roots. In the main, the more exciting activities were
taking place on the fringes rather than in the crazy hurly-burly of the
showcase maelstrom around 6th Street and Red River.

Examples of such gems were the unfortunately-named Mother
Truckers, playing a blinder to celebrate carrying off the Austin
Music Roots Award; or Graham Parker, storming along with New
York power trio the Figgs, or Canadian future stars Luke Doucet,
Melissa McLelland and Justin Rutledge forming an impromptu
mini-supergroup and almost blowing the roof off Headhunters.

I have to note that the UK presence was a huge curate's egg. On
the first night, the Texan audience listened in disbelief to the facile
Eurovision style performance by the inept Lily Allen and her dire
band. Her idea of entertaining the Yanks was to slag off the NME.
Razorlight cheered things up with their usual bravado, Johnny
Borrell's Jaggeresque mannerisms stopping just short of self-parody.
In the trouser department, he might just as well go the whole hog
and adopt the see-through kecks of Iggy Pop (also present at SXSW
as a Stooge).

Across the weekend, numerous performances by Amy Winehouse
justly made her the talk of the town. Opinions differed on The

Good, The Bad And The Queen but I found their languid bass-heavy whimsy perfect for the wee hours.

The notion of corporate sponsorship has now developed into government support with merch-heavy Welsh, Scottish and English Showcases succeeding in clashing with each other. A quick dash between them didn't reveal much: The Automatic (frantic pop), The Fratellis (less frantic pop) and Mica (um … Gilbert O'Sullivan?). Much more to my taste were more genuine, less-hyped acts such as Raleigh's intense and ever-entertaining Patty Hurst Shifter, the Drams (rocking former Slobberboners from Denton), the magnificently noisy Austinites Grand Champeen, the moody Sparklehorse (sadly plagued by sound problems) and the increasingly energetic and accessible Deadstring Brothers from Detroit. Not to forget a charming highlight in the form of Buzzcocks, playing a rampant greatest hits set to a demented audience.

It was fitting that the festival should close with fiery performances from two sets of local boys, Friends Of Dean Martinez with their moody instrumental soundscapes, and Midlake, who made it to Band of SXSW 2007 for me by demonstrating their intelligence and originality in a short but emotionally performed and received set. Music from the heart, that's what SXSW is all about.

This was a year in which my outlets were restricted to short pieces in the Chronicle and Record Collector, so couldn't go into much detail. It was, however, a year with performances that had tragic ramifications. Both Mark Linkous and Amy Winehouse were destined to die within a few years in tragic and deeply upsetting circumstances.

VENUE SPOTLIGHT: EMO'S

Situated at the busy intersection between Red River and Sixth Street, Emo's was, until recently, when it changed its name and policies, the quintessential Austin venue. With four rooms and an outside courtyard with a large stage, it was a favourite venue for high-profile showcases, but all suffered badly from sound leakage from one room to the next, plus, of course, the traditional terrible toilets that all venues in this part of town boast. I first visited Emo's in search of the British band Field Music, whose management had asked me in my rôle at Amplifier to do a review and feature on them. As they were starting out as a new band, their quiet Englishness, respectable short hair and freshly ironed trousers looked dramatically out of place in this down-at-heel environment. Emo's has been the scene of a lot of musical adventures for me, probably the most exciting one being wandering in the footsteps of Amy Winehouse as she strode the streets, tottering around in her high heels, seemingly without any security but with a permanent small gaggle of fans trotting alongside her. At Emo's she was hobnobbing with Steve Diggle of Buzzcocks and dancing away to them in the front row. Another unforgettable Emo's memory was experiencing a long and very good set from Jimmy Cliff. As a big fan of reggae in general and his film The Harder They Come specifically, I thought he would be the coolest dude in town, and indeed he was. The problem was that his rather baggy, bright red trousers had the fly zip undone for the entire hour-long set and I feared a dramatic wardrobe malfunction as he danced around the stage. It was almost tempting to beckon him to the front and whisper the shame into his ear, but I didn't dare. On another occasion, I had an embarrassing encounter at Emo's with The Vaccines, who were at the start of their career and very much the cool new thing. For complicated reasons, I knew their drummer, who had played in my daughter's band previously, so I was relatively confident as I strode up to them to say hello. Pete the drummer was admirably friendly but the other guys in the band were visibly shocked to see him nattering with this strange and boring old git, who certainly was not the kind of cool person they wished to be seen interacting with. It was a slightly strained encounter. As the focus of South By Southwest moved ever further away from 6th Street, Emo's began to lose its cachet and is now a different venue altogether, but warm memories are evoked whenever I walk past its hulk.

BANDS SEEN IN 2007

Lily Allen
Buzzcocks
The Deadstring Brothers
Dolorean
The Drams
The Figgs
The Flaming Lips
The Fratellis
David Garza
The Good, The Bad & The Queen
Mark Mallman
Ox
Graham Parker
Patty Hurst Shifter
Sparklehorse
Jesse Sykes & The Sweet Hereafter
Amy Winehouse

YEAR 6: 2008 / MARCH 11 - 15

Distilled from reviews in the Hampshire Chronicle
and Record Collector.

It was while watching the remarkable Micah P. Hinson in action that
I realized I had a theme for this year's South By Southwest festival.
He introduced a song by explaining that he wrote it in London's
Union Chapel in honour of his engagement. As he smiled shyly at
his fiancée in the front row, the song resonated with pure, loving
emotion.

Having sprained my ankle the day before leaving, there was no
question of the traditional charging around searching for hot new
acts, so instead I decided to spend time with artists I already knew
and could rely on to be great. Several of them featured a male-
female duo of front-persons who are partners in real life. Canada's
Luke Doucet and Melissa McClelland are both solo artists, but now
teamed as Luke Doucet and the White Falcon, their joint shows
sparkled with good humour, love and musical brilliance. The same is
true of Detroit's Deadstring Brothers. Since Masha Marjieh stepped
up to share vocal duties with partner Kurt Marschke, this band, with
a little help from their English friends, has been transformed into a
rocking powerhouse like the Faces fronted by Tina Turner. You get
the feeling they are on the cusp of much greater recognition. *(Ahem,
Masha and Kurt promptly split up and the band imploded, never to
be heard of again.)*

Chuck Prophet and the Mission Express also feature a partnership.

With Chuck cajoling, teasing and encouraging Stephanie Finch to ever more prominence in the band, it was charming to watch this shy person's amazement and joy at the affection the audience showed her. So fantastic musically and personally were all three of these acts that I went to see all of them twice.

It was impossible to entirely resist doing a bit of chasing (or hobbling) after the hot new acts, though, and a pretty mixed bunch they were. Surely the Americans will have more sense than to fall for the bland Duffy, who made you want to cry "Bring back Bonnie Tyler". Then there were the dozens of wham-bam indie outfits propping up the showcase gigs, of whom only two stood out: the extremely cool Rascals, who feature a mini-Lennon with great attitude (Miles Kane) and the cheerful Scouting for Girls, whose Roy Stride may well have a future of Elton John proportions.

Austin's Okkervil River celebrated their breakthrough with an epic set at Stubb's, while Southend's These New Puritans took the prize for daftest shirt and Lightspeed Champion bordered on the unconvincing, with just acoustic guitar and fiddle being unable to do justice to the songs.

Returning to the sexual chemistry theme, two acts that exploited it rather than letting it speak for herself came head-to-head, but it was no contest. The Raveonettes remained resolutely monotonous while The Kills crackled with static. And let's not forget the ubiquitous Sons And Daughters, whose Adele and Scott are partners too. What has rock and roll come to? A hotbed of contented domesticity, it would seem, and none the worse for it.

Another year with limited outlets and reduced coverage. There were plenty of other highlights though. Dead Rock West was (still is) a duo of two intriguing and lovable characters called Frank Lee Drennen and Cindy Wassermann, yet another affectionate and enigmatic combo who can rock out hard when required. Roky Erikson's presence in town was a big deal for Austinites. A Texan native famous for his psychedelic experiments, brushes with the law and his band the 13th Floor Elevators, he was performing with the help of local band Okkervill River, and succeeded in packing out Stubb's for a rocking, if mildly uncoordinated show.

One person I did correctly identify at sxsw as a tip for the top was Miles Kane, now a successful solo star and member of The Last Shadow Puppets with Alex Turner of Arctic Monkeys (about whom I had been less complimentary). His trio The Rascals (as opposed to The Young Rascals) put in a stormingly cheeky little set, largely ignored by the schmoozy industry-dominated daytime showcase audience. Looking at some laminates, I found I was standing next to music journalist Chris Welch, whom I had last seen while co-covering the Reading Festival with him in 1980. Chris had been the deputy editor of Musicians Only while I worked for them but we never really got on and I didn't say hello for fear of being rebuffed.

The brevity of the Bands Seen list must be down to my lack of mobility that year. One thing I say to people planning to attend SXSW is that they do need to be fit, because the public transport system (excellent though it is) will not be much help.

Patty Hurst Shifter was a great name for a fine band with an impressive pedigree. Drummer Skillet Gilmore had been a member of Whiskeytown along with his wife Caitlin Cary, Ryan Adams and Philip Wandscher, whom we'd seen the year before with Jesse Sykes. At the heart of Patty Hurst Shifter were two brothers called J Chris Smith and Marc E Smith. It was tempting to call out for Fall songs to the latter, but for Paul and me the main attraction was cheerful bassist Jesse Huebner, who bore an uncanny resemblance to Harry Enfield. Not being familiar with Harry's oeuvre, Jesse was perpetually baffled by the two of us shoving wads of dollars in his face while bellowing "LOADSAMONEY!!!" Through the medium of Facebook, I have stayed in touch with all four members of PHS, even though the band is no more. Caitlin and Skillet run a craft shop in Raleigh, North Carolina.

Sons And Daughters were a classic example of me going over the top in plugging a band that subsequently fizzled out without making an impact, but The Kills are still going and are as cool as ever. Scouting For Girls didn't have quite the stellar future I was *predicting but nonethless continue to appear on mid-range festival bills each summer.*

One complete mystery is why I didn't mention REM in the review, considering they played at Stubb's and I remember squeezing in at the last moment and viewing them from a great distance at the top of the hill. But their jangly sound was quintessential SXSW late Saturday night, mildly intoxicated joy.

VENUE FOCUS: MARIA'S TACO EXPRESS

Tears were shed in 2020 when the glorious institution that was Maria's Taco Express finally bowed to the inevitable and sold out to a development company. Originally set up as a food truck on South Lamar in 1997, this was a local venue with a large patio and covered stage that functioned mainly as a restaurant for the rest of the year but always attracted large numbers of bands during South By Southwest week. Situated next door to a branch of Walgreens with a particularly brutal car parking policy, it wasn't that easy to access, but once inside, levels of cosiness were achieved that were unrivalled elsewhere in the showcase scene. For close on a decade, Maria's hosted line-ups curated by the much-loved and super-stylish Austin musician Alejandro Escovedo, who was able to pull all sorts of strings to ensure extremely high quality performances. I remember once getting tremendously excited when Alexandro told me he was going to introduce me to his manager. I knew that at the time Alejandro's manager was Jon Landau, who also managed Bruce Springsteen, but in the event, the person I was introduced to turned out to be a member of his team. That was the same day when I thought I'd gone mad because I recognized Ed Tree, the guitarist in the American version of the Spencer Davis Group, whom I'd been talking to only a few days previously in Sydney, Australia.

I have enjoyed some fantastic entertainment at Maria's over the years. For someone like me, being generally quite restrained in behaviour, it's quite something to start downing Margaritas and chips with burning hot salsa at midday. Dang, those Margaritas, which of course emerge from a large plastic crushed ice machine, are potent and tasty. They immediately have that terrifying effect of making you think that you're dying of a brain aneurism because the ice has induced an agonising pain in the front of your head. There is a way to cure this, but I can never remember it at the vital moment. Among performances I have seen at Maria's, several have been uniquely memorable. The magnificently entertaining Jesse Malin loves to do wild forays into the audience and on one charming occasion, he incorporated a young lad with special needs who was in the front row into the stage act. It was delightful and hugely endearing.

Maria's was also the first place I saw a performance by another unique artist, BP Fallon. Better known for his decades as a PR supremo, representing the likes of T-Rex, Led Zeppelin, etc, Beep, as he is affectionately known, is tiny of stature and quite riveting as a personality, with his little bowler hat, his sparkling eyes and his bald pate. Not much of a singer, he instead prefers to recite his lyrics and because he is so legendary, he has access to some incredible musicians such as Austin's own rampant duo the Ghost Wolves or Joe King Carrasco and the Crowns. Of all the places that have closed down in Austin over the years, Maria's is the one I miss the most.

BANDS SEEN IN 2008

Billy Bragg
Dead Rock West
The Deadstring Brothers
Luke Doucet & Melissa McClelland
Duffy
Elliott Brood
Roky Erikson
Micah P Hinson
Mark Mallman
NQ Arbuckle

Okkervill River
Patty Hurst Shifter
Chuck Prophet & The Mission Express
R.E.M.
The Rascals
Johnathan Rice
Scouting For Girls
These New Puritans

YEAR 7: 2009 / MARCH 17 - 21

Distilled from reviews in the Hampshire Chronicle
and Record Collector.

You might not think Winchester would have much influence on a worldwide music convention like South By Southwest in Austin, Texas but you'd be surprised. For a start, much curiosity greeted the post-Andy Burrows version of Razorlight. What would they be like? Dire, was the answer. Without Andy's sparkling personality and inspired drumming, they came across as completely washed-up, slinking off stage to silence after just 25 minutes. They're in big trouble.

Other Hampshire artists were a little less prominent. I had trouble tracking down (and even spelling) Dlugokecki, who was supposed to be in attendance. Frank Turner, by contrast, was ubiquitous, but I avoided him as (whisper it), I don't particularly rate him. Winchester's Chris T-T, a fine live performer, had the proverbial nightmare. Given a graveyard slot in an inappropriate venue, he suffered from a malfunctioning borrowed guitar but still managed to gain an encore – a rarity at SXSW.

You could easily write a book about this festival (ahem) but the madness of SXSW can be summed up by a crazy afternoon presented by Mojo magazine in a patio venue on the edge of town called the Mean Eyed Cat. Here you could experience, in quick succession, veteran popstars The Proclaimers, operatic Texan shoegazers Shearwater, the glam rock of Justin Hawkins' post-Darkness pastiche

Hot Leg, some unlistenable thrash metal band and the dark acoustic ballads of the Handsome Family.

Ah, the Mean Eyed Cat. Those really were the days. Simply being present at the Mean Eyed Cat bashes felt extremely rock and roll because not many people found their way there, yet the lineups were always stellar and the kudos of being associated with Mojo magazine was another bonus. The shows were curated by British Underground in London, who had all the requisite contacts to put together stunning bills. It must have been sponsored by someone too, because there were always copious lashings of free beer, something that isn't necessarily a given at every showcase. The Mean Eyed Cat, way out in the suburbs, had a delightfully down-at-heel, seedy vibe into which most of the artists fitted perfectly. I have this abiding memory of leaving the venue and following down the street a still fully stage-clothed Justin Hawkins of The Darkness, whose band Hot Leg had just played. With his flares flapping and his beads jangling, he attracted astonished looks from all around, yet strode along briskly and confidently in the way that only a true rock star can.

Triumph of the week was a towering performance from PJ Harvey and John Parish, which completely animated the same audience which had just been so deflated by Razorlight. The screaming adulation and thinking back to the early days of their collaboration playing as Automatic Dlamini in the back room of Winchester's Railway Inn was inspirational.

This was a year to be mildly troubled by noticing the ageing process in admired performers. The previously svelte and super-cool Gerard Langley of Bristol's Blue Aeroplanes had developed a paunch, was losing his hair and needed a music stand from which to read his poetry (nowadays it would be an iPad on a stick). The band, famous for having at least three or more guitarists, was reduced to an economical four-piece and thus was minus much of its uniqueness. Similarly, Pete Murphy of Bauhaus was demonstrating the difficulty of growing old as a Goth, sporting a Bobby Charlton-style combover complemented by a long, straggly mullet. Not that appearances are everything, of course – Lord knows I'm not immune to the ravages of age – but in rock and roll, image is an integral part of the whole and can't be ignored.

Clocking in as still able to carry off an image were the inimitable Primal Scream. I have a strong memory of a scene I observed at the busy junction of 6th and Red River, where a circle had formed round Mani and Bobby Gillespie as they stood in the middle of the road, trying to work out where they were going. Most of the spectators would have had no idea who they were, but one thing was for sure – they had the unmistakable aura of true rock stars.

VENUE SPOTLIGHT: STUBB'S

Stubb's Bar-B-Q is Austin's premier venue and one of the few outside ones. On first visiting, you will be struck by the fact that it's a health and safety nightmare, because it's built on a relatively steep slope and the surface is gravel with random boulders here and there. Drink outlets are scattered around the edges and the stage is at the bottom of the valley, creating an amphitheatre feel. It's a historic venue with extremely high production facilities, which is why the major acts appearing at South By Southwest each year will be found at Stubb's.

I have seen scores of performances here of wildly varying quality. One of the worst was the Welsh singer Duffy, who struggled to stay in tune as the crowds drifted away en masse, but I forgave her on learning, years later, about how appallingly she was treated by the music industry. Other impressive acts we've seen at Stubb's include Nick Cave, The Pretenders, The Specials and a really captivating effort by The Good, The Bad and The Queen, a short-lived project featuring Paul Simonon and Damon Albarn.

We discovered early on that there is a secret way to get right to the stage front by sneaking down a narrow passageway behind the beer stands on the left, which brings you out right by the photographers' pit. If you can be on the barrier there, you can have an outstanding front row experience. This was at its most intense for me when seeing PJ Harvey and John Parish in 2009. Such is the nature of Polly Harvey fans that people were fainting and hyperventilating all around us.

It's certainly not a place for anyone with claustrophobia issues as, despite the carefully-controlled entrance procedures, it can get very overcrowded. Although Stubb's has a relatively high capacity, the demand for the bigger acts is often far more than can be accommodated, leading to huge queues stretching for hundreds of metres along Red River Street. You need to get there extremely early or judge when to give up even trying to get in.

Directly opposite Stubb's there used to be a mediocre Tex-Mex restaurant called Jaime's Spanish Kitchen. When we first saw it, Paul and I doubted its advertised claim to be the best Mexican food in Austin. In typical in-joke style, we never referred to it by its real name, merely as 'the most magnificent restaurant in the entire history of the universe'. It was a convenient place to eat prior to delving into the mayhem of Stubb's. One year, we arranged to meet Razorlight drummer Andy Burrows there. Andy has always had the enviable ability to drink large amounts of lager before going on stage without any detrimental effect on his performance, and so it was on this occasion.

Another time, I invited the entire PJ Harvey Band out for dinner there. I must have been drinking because I certainly couldn't afford to do so, but once I had issued the invitation I could hardly backtrack. The band members, especially drummer Jean-Marc, are highly sophisticated people with good tastes in cuisine and I could tell from their faces that they were unconvinced by Jaime's claims of culinary magnificence. I tried to appear casual when looking at the bill but nearly suffered an internal nervous breakdown.

This may be a good place to reflect upon my relationship with Andy Burrows. We saw Razorlight three times over the years in Austin, once prior to Andy joining, once while he was in the band

and once after he left. The only time they were any good was when he was with them. Still, it's a heartwarming story. Andy grew up in my home town of Winchester and I have known him since he was in his early teens, supporting his efforts in a series of worthy bands with names such as User, Stag and Moja, the last of which also featured Sir Tim Rice's daughter Eva, because she was in a relationship with Pete Hobbs, who was in the former two bands. I was concerned about Andy's future, as none of these ventures met with any success. He was also enduring a tough time as his parents went through a difficult divorce, but then, in time-honoured fashion, Andy answered an ad and auditioned for Razorlight when their previous drummer Christian Smith-Pancorvo left them.

Andy was bringing a lot more to Razorlight than they realised, as he went on to write or co-write a number of their major hits, including the worldwide smash America. His famously volatile relationship with singer Johnny Borrell always made for an exciting stage atmosphere. Nowadays Andy lives a rockstar lifestyle in a manor house in the Cotswolds, close to where I grew up, and somehow we have remained firm pals through thick and thin.

Similarly, the reason for me being on such familiar terms with the PJ Harvey band dates back to my longstanding friendship with their leader John Parish, whom I first met in 1979 when he auditioned for Thieves Like Us, the band that I managed at the time. Just like with Andy, we have managed to stay in touch in all the subsequent decades as John has gone on to become one of the world's most respected and successful record producers, as well as close collaborator and musical director for Polly Harvey. I still wish I hadn't had to pay that bill though.

BANDS SEEN IN 2009

And You Will Know Us By The Trail Of Dead
Asteroids Galaxy Tour
Black Lips

The Blue Aeroplanes
The Decemberists
Delta Spirit
Luke Doucet and Melissa McLelland
Elliott Brood
The Handsome Family
PJ Harvey & John Parish
Hot Leg
Lightspeed Champion
Jason Lytle
Pete Murphy
NQ Arbuckle
Primal Scream
Razorlight
Shearwater
Shout Out Out Out Out
The Soft Pack
Chris T-T
Justin Townes Earle

YEAR 8: 2010 / MARCH 16 - 20

Distilled from reviews in the Hampshire Chronicle,
Record Collector and Caught In The Act.

*A new way of commentating on SXSW presented itself this year. It was
sparked by the renewal of an acquaintance with some music media
people I had worked with a lot in the 1970s and 80s. Stick It In Your
Ear was a cassette-only music label based in Southampton, and they
also had their own in-house magazine. After many years of SIIYE
dormancy, proprietor Geoff Wall retired from his job at the Ordnance
Survey and set up a unique online music magazine called Caught In
The Act. The purpose of it is stated as providing the opportunity
for long-form music writing and, uniquely, it specifically declares
to its writers that they have no word limit. It has developed into a
highly intellectual, dare I say almost nerdy forum where, just like in
Record Collector, there are no musical boundaries or conventions
and numerous different genres are covered by a selection of very
gifted writers. I offered my services to Geoff. He encouraged me to
contribute and my annual SXSW coverage for CITA has now become
a tradition. This is why, as you read this book, you will suddenly find
from now on that all the reviews become enormously lengthy and
possibly unnecessarily detailed.*

TUESDAY

I never have problems sleeping, except on one day each year. That
is the day when I travel to Austin for South By Southwest. The route

this year is Southampton - Manchester - Chicago - Austin, and the flight is very early in the morning. I have booked a taxi and set the alarm, so that should be sufficient, but no. What if the alarm fails to go off? What if the taxi driver's alarm doesn't go off and he fails to turn up? Best not to risk going to sleep then, but in this case it's immaterial, because I have such a savage cough that sleep is out of the question anyway.

That cough. For days, I've been worrying on behalf of whatever poor person will have to sit next to me on the eight-hour transatlantic flight. Now I am sure I have the solution. I have bought a bottle of cough mixture and cleverly decanted most of it so that less than 30 ml is left. Unfortunately that cuts no ice with the officials at Southampton Airport, who insist it is thrown away. They assure me, though I don't believe it, that cough mixture is on sale in the duty free shop.

Astonishingly, I am wrong, and purchase a replacement bottle which enables me to spare my germs from the businessmen who make up the entire passenger list of the commuter flight to Manchester. I look around and confirm that I am the only person present who is not wearing a suit. I feel rather smug that my next few days are not going to be as dull as theirs will be.

Transferring to the next flight makes you feel good, as you are fast-tracked to the front of the queue. To my relief, the security official doesn't make me throw away the cough mixture again, and I board the plane. This time last year, it was a huge jumbo which allowed me to stretch out across three seats, just behind Jarvis Cocker, who was doing the same. This plane, however, is much smaller and inevitably I am squashed next to someone of enormous girth who spills over on to my seat. Boarding is an hour late because - get this - the incoming flight has had to be diverted round Iceland because of an erupting volcano. Then, we sit for a further hour and a half while engineers try to supply the plane with water, not for the radiator as I naively assumed (I guess jet planes don't have radiators), but for the loos and the tea. In the event, the tea tastes as if the water came from the loo anyway. My handy pocket book of crosswords comes in useful in passing the time, in contrast to two truly terrible Ricky Gervais Hollywood films which are played back to back on the neckache-inducing screens.

The lateness means a quick stopover in Chicago and before I know it I'm in Austin, where Paul collects me from the airport.

WEDNESDAY

It dawns warm and sunny, and my cough is in full retreat as we stroll from our conveniently-situated Super 8 Motel along Red River and towards the Convention Center.

My request for the afternoon was to re-visit a place I went to with Birgit when she and I first visited Austin ten years ago. The Oasis is an extraordinary restaurant built into a series of decks overlooking Lake Travis. It recently burned down and is in the process of being rebuilt as something much more posh. We chomped burgers and revelled in the sunshine. I couldn't believe I'd forgotten the sunscreen.

That was it for the car. From now on, beer was going to be a major part of our diet, so the car remained behind and it was down to feet and the very occasional taxi in time of need. Just for the record, I am suffering (again) from a very painful foot. This kicked in more or less immediately and remained agonising throughout the four days, so anything I describe as 'walking' should actually read 'hobbling'. This is significant, as any visit to SXSW entails many, many miles on foot.

I'm going to attempt to describe the scene. At first glance, everything seems reasonably reachable. There is a slew of venues on Sixth Street, and on thoroughfares like Red River, which cross it. There is nothing to stop you just staying in this temporarily pedestrianised area, the most crowded, but you'd miss out on an awful lot if you did. Some bigger venues, such as the open air one at Town Lake, and also La Zona Rosa and the Austin Music Hall are quite a serious hike away. Here is where some big names are likely to appear (examples this year being Smokey Robinson and Ray

Davies), but we have bitter experience of long journeys followed by fruitless hours standing in queues, and now ignore these events. Some of the best shows are in venues such as Opal Divine's or the Continental Club, both of which are a long way from the main action. A few places, such as the improvised venues on South Congress (Home Slice Pizza, Yard Dog Gallery), the Mean Eyed Cat and the Hole in The Wall (out by the university) are actually quite a hefty taxi ride, but normally worth the effort. One or two bars (very few indeed) actually choose to opt out of SXSW altogether:

The badges and wristbands don't actually guarantee you entry to anything. During the day parties, you can go almost anywhere you like and, with patience, will get to see virtually any band, because they all play several shows, some managing as many as ten or more over the four days. The main difficulty is finding out who is playing where and when. The officially documented events are the teeniest tip of the iceberg.

Sometimes you will find out what's happening because you are on a particular band's mailing list. Sometimes there are posters that give you clues. Word of mouth is very active, plus nowadays there are all sorts of social networking devices that I don't comprehend. Sometimes you can strike lucky by spotting a long queue and attaching yourself to it. One thing which it is worth ignoring is when word gets out that a big, unbilled band is playing in a small place (this year, it was Muse at Stubb's). You are in severe danger of standing in the queue for five or six hours, missing a load of other good stuff, and still not getting in.

There's no way to solve the problem of awful clashes. When you search the schedules, you sometimes find a certain time when there is absolutely no one you want to see, followed an hour later by five or more acts you are desperate to see, all playing at the same time in different places. Or, in a variation on the theme, someone at six o'clock followed by someone else at seven o'clock but unfortunately five miles away. If you're not careful, you catch the first few songs of Act A (you know, the unfamiliar ones from their new album), miss the rousing climax and arrive at Act B just in time to catch the immortal words "Thank you, goodnight" (they always say goodnight even if it's mid-afternoon). You then listen to the crowd discussing what an incredibly brilliant set you have just missed.

I started SXSW 2010 in the same way as usual, at the Canadian Blast, which takes place in a tent in Brush Park outside the Convention Center. Canadian music is government-supported and usually this event is great, but this year I was unfortunate enough to encounter a series of rather nondescript bands, with the exception of You Say Party! We Say Die!, who were actually quite good, but I couldn't take them seriously because their singer reminded me too much of Miss Jones from Rising Damp.

It was time to head to Lambert's, a far-flung upstairs venue which is actually a smart restaurant in normal life. Here you can find the most expensive beer of any SXSW venue, although it is very good beer. By contrast, the toilet was one of the very worst (and there's lots of competition). Mark Mallman was performing here with his other band, bouncy electro-poppers Ruby Isle. I wanted to talk to Mark about a possible UK tour, but the news was bad. The proposed fee for a small UK show would mean a big deficit for Mark, and he doesn't have record company support. Despite that disappointment, the show was great and Mark is always ideal for a good photo opportunity.

Opal Divine's is a long way from Lambert's but I had promised to visit Welsh singer-songwriter Christopher Rees, who was excited to be playing with the South Austin Horns. It was a 'flying by the seat of the pants' show, but a nervous Christopher came across really well with a soulful performance, quite different from his normal more country stylings. The only problems were the lugubrious concentration of the sidemen and the almost complete lack of an audience. I had to set off before the end on a hike to see someone who, no offence, beat the horns hands down in the beauty stakes.

Asteroids Galaxy Tour is a Danish band we stumbled upon by chance at last year's SXSW. Their claim to fame is having their tune Around The Bend used in a TV commercial for Apple, but they are fantastic fun, with the stunning Mette Lindberg backed by what amounts to a soul band, complete with a decadent-looking horn section. They are great entertainment but you wonder what the future holds for them. It's a miracle that industry types haven't tried to transform Mette into a Gaga-style electro-Diva, but she seems the sort of person who wouldn't take kindly to attempted manipulation.

Just up the road is Club De Ville and my next plan was to see a band I'd wanted to see for a while, namely Bowerbirds. It turned out to be an object lesson in the Unacceptable Face Of SXSW. It doesn't happen often, but when it does, it's infuriating. Along with a couple of hundred other people, I stood for over an hour as a completely hopeless excuse for a sound crew failed to enable the extraordinarily patient band to conduct a sound check. The crew were communicating over the PA, which revealed that they genuinely had no more clue what they were doing than most of the crowd would have had. Along with many other people, I eventually gave up and left without hearing a note, sad that we had potentially missed something better round the corner. That's why I was headed to Stubb's, to try and get in early for Austin's finest (equal) band, Spoon. It was a big deal for them to be headlining the prestige venue and they pulled it off with aplomb, aided by the fact that they only have a few members and instruments and therefore don't need complicated sound checks. Plus, bless them, they do a sweetly lugubrious cover of the Damned classic 'Love Song'. As usual at Stubb's, we nipped down the secret side alley and got a deafening ringside view and the traditional telling-off from the bouncers for using flash photography. Well, it's not my fault if I don't know how to turn the flash off.

THURSDAY

Yesterday, I had made the embarrassing error of heading to a Shearwater show 24 hours early, having mis-read the schedule. The Galaxy Rooms is a strange place which seems to change hands and name each year. It is currently up for sale and completely empty, which actually makes it great for gig-going. They have brought in a stage and a PA, which is pretty much all you need. I make no bones about adoring Shearwater (prog roots revealed) and they delivered as usual. They all look so blissfully happy, it's no wonder the music comes out so brilliantly. In the wrong hands it could be pompous, but as it is, it's sublime.

The afternoon panned out in perfect style. At two, we were at Headhunters for the Six Shooter Hootenanny. With free Tequila and lovely tacos, the atmosphere is fantastic and the music great. Each act does just a couple of numbers and lots of cross-pollination goes on. Each year, I find something new and fun here, and this year it was Edmonton's Hot Panda.

What could possibly drag us away from the Hootenanny? Probably the best band of the festival, that's what, namely Rhode Island's The Low Anthem, who had triumphed at the End Of The Road Festival back in September, and who triumphed again at the Galaxy Rooms. How lovely that such quiet, slow, intelligent music can hold an audience so rapt amidst all the mayhem on the streets outside.

I was on a mission by now, doubtless fuelled by the Tequila, and needed to see one of my favourite artists, Jason Lytle (previously of Grandaddy). Lytle famously hated the pressures of fame and now has gone so far as to assimilate himself anonymously into a band called Admiral Radley, which played six times during the festival. Unfortunately we chose the wrong show because (are you seeing a pattern here?) they had trouble sound checking and by the time they got going, only had time for three songs, ignominiously playing behind a flickering projection of a sponsors' logo. But I would later encounter Jason again.

After a quick peek at the excellent Besnard Lakes at Stubb's, I was off on a hunch. John Parish had recommended Nive Nielsen, a singer from Greenland, to my knowledge, the only artist from that country ever to play at SXSW. Also, she was playing on the eighteenth floor of the Hilton Garden Inn, where I like to go at least once a year for a rest from excessive volume. Nive was enjoyable but suffered from a condition afflicting many this year, namely an inability to resist using a raft of unnecessary backing musicians. Many of the songs got lost in the convoluted arrangements and it was always a relief when she did something solo. Plus, oh dear, it entailed very lengthy soundchecking.

Everyone says how brilliant the Drive By Truckers are, so in the spirit of supporting local music, we headed back to Stubb's. Last time I saw them I found them to be lumbering, bog-standard alt-country with few redeeming features, and this time I found them to be - er - lumbering, bog-standard alt-country with few redeeming features. Surrounded by a crowd of Truckers fans, we survived five songs before heading off to a far more important Texan band.

Centro-Matic have been a highlight of all the 'South Bys' I have attended apart from last year's, when they unaccountably didn't play. After the disappointment of the cancellation of Will Johnson's tour with Jason Molina (owing to Molina's illness), it was essential to see them this time and, of course, they never disappoint. Even in the characterless tented Emo's Annexe, the trenchant rock and Johnson's soulful vocals underlined their uniqueness. It was terribly sobering when Johnson dedicated one song to the memories of Alex Chilton, Vic Chesnutt and Mark Linkous. That is way too many dead geniuses in a short time.

Buffalo Billiards is normally one of my favourite SXSW venues. Situated upstairs, it tends to host the hottest shows. This was where I rushed to after Centro-Matic, to catch another bunch of heroes from Denton, namely Midlake. Surprisingly, there was no queue, but a musical problem for me. Despite their 'The Courage Of Others' being one of my top albums of 2010, they also suffered from having too many extra members. Because most of their instruments, including non-rock and roll items such as flutes, are acoustic, they - guess what - soundchecked forever and then gave a muted and, oh dear, rather boring performance. Oh well, bed time anyway.

FRIDAY

This is a good moment to add that the bands mentioned here are only a sample of those we saw. Nipping in and out of bars, you catch snatches of scores of acts you never identify, plus others you fail to remember. And while it isn't really a street festival, you do come across gems on street corners, such as the Coal Porters, playing their hearts out outside a bank on Sixth Street.

Whenever I am at South By Southwest, I have to keep my eyes open for Hampshire bands, so it was with a certain amount of joy, not to mention surprise, that I spotted in the programme a reference to Southampton. What's this? Band Of Skulls? God, it sounds like some horrible hardcore band, but I'd better investigate.

Investigation proved fruitful. They sounded great, they seemed respected and they were about to tour with Black Rebel Motorcycle Club. But - my blood ran cold - it seemed I knew them after all. It dawned on me that this was a band previously known as Fleeing New York, about whom I had once written a stinking review. Now I may not have been wrong about that particular band, but obviously things had changed in a major way. So in Austin, I was determined to find Band Of Skulls and make amends. The show I had decided upon (out of several) was to take place at the Cedar Street Courtyard at 1 pm, an outrageously early time by SXSW standards, but there was a problem. There was only one queue, and it was plain that hundreds of hopefuls were employing my 'get there early' technique in order to see Black Rebel Motorcycle Club, scheduled for later in the afternoon.

On this occasion, someone had decided to roll all the queues into one, which was not exactly fair for people like me, who not only had a badge but had also gone through a lengthy online rigmarole to reply to an invitation and acquire a confirmation. Well, I'm not proud, but I wasn't going to miss this band, so, in an entirely uncharacteristic Tequila-fuelled attack of bravery / aggression, I barged past the doorman and strode into the crowd before anyone could stop me, rather startling the smartly-dressed delegation from the Hamburg Reeperbahn festival, whose promotional stall I knocked over in the process.

The reward was ample, though. Sneaking through the side bar to prime position in the front row, I felt a warm glow of pride as the compère announced that he was an Austin radio DJ and that Band Of

Skulls was the most requested band on his station. A Southampton band making it big in the States? How exciting is this? And how could it be? Well, how it can be is that this is not just a band name change, it's an entirely new and very American sound. You know how the White Stripes and the Black Keys have that spare, bluesy earthiness but sometimes you wish they had a bass player? That's the trick that Band of Skulls pull off. Bassist Emma Richardson looks and sounds great, cool in a Hynde way but somehow rather English Rose-like. Guitarist Russell Marsden is more unkempt but wrestles out abrasive squalls of sound and makes a grand job of that most excellent rock and roll tradition of kneeling on the floor, extracting groans and screeches from his effects pedals. Plus drummer Matthew Hayward, with his minimalist style, outshone at least a thousand other drummers in town. The hooks on many of the songs are almost chants, simple yet not obvious. Wow! For a second, I toyed with shouting out "Go Southampton!" at the end of the set, but resisted, for fear of being branded a football hooligan. And I chickened out of trying to speak to them. If I had, I would have apologized for my age-old petulance, of course.

I had already booked (on spec) Sarah Borges and the Broken Singles to play in Winchester, so wanted to make sure it had been a good idea. The Belmont is one of the most salubrious SXSW venues, and I have to admit that, chilling on the patio in the blazing sunshine, eating a 'cone of shrimps' and nursing a Dos Equis (the most glorious Mexican beer), I felt all was very good in the world. So it was that, when I spotted the notoriously shy and un-showbizzy Jason Lytle in the crowd, I simply marched up and started talking to him. I don't know what came over me, that's just what SXSW does to you. Luckily, the mood seemed to have got to him too and he was charm personified, allowing me to feel that I hadn't entirely made a fool of myself. Sarah Borges was great, too, so visiting the Belmont was a good result all round.

Paul, meanwhile, had adored The Low Anthem so much that he insisted on trying to get in to what turned out to be a private media showcase, and had lengthy and unfruitful negotiations with an unbending security team. So we met up again to try to get to the Hole In The Wall, a distant venue where Chuck Prophet and the Mission Express were playing the first of their many shows. The taxi we eventually found was driven by a militantly gay chain smoker, maybe not the kind of thing people associate with Texas, but this is Austin. On the return journey, however, the driver was an outspoken and vile homophobe. Ho hum.

The Chuck show here was intensely vibrant, maybe not one of their tidiest (he told me afterwards that he "didn't know what the hell was going on") but with all the unique excitement that a full-on Mission Express show can stir up. Here, as all over town, the spirit of Alex Chilton was palpably present. Alex had been billed to play at Antones with Big Star but sadly passed away in New Orleans on the Wednesday. Chilton songs are often a feature of Chuck Prophet shows and this was no exception.

A long walk later, it was time to hit the Central Presbyterian Church, one of several ecclesiastical venues brought into SXSW service. Just as well we arrived early, because they can't just pack more and more people into the pews, so there is a more finite capacity than elsewhere. A long and friendly queueing procedure (with no alcohol or loos available) was eventually rewarded by Band Of Horses, playing melodic, Eagles-ish music which seemed entirely appropriate. Hard on the bum though.

For some reason, I thought it would be a good idea to see Boxer Rebellion at Maggie Mae's but I was wrong, as they turned out to be a bombastic, sub-Muse affair. Entertainment was to be had, though, observing one gentleman pouring beer from the balcony into the upturned mouth of his mate on the ground floor below, with quite impressive accuracy. It seemed like an ideal opportunity to get early into the line for the Red Eyed Fly, a venue where queuing is dangerous because it is in a busy car park. Fruitless, too, on this occasion, as after forty minutes of immobility it was clear we were never going to get in to see Deer Tick. So it was time to trouble the shoe leather again in a challenging trek to the Continental Club. This is one of the most atmospheric Austin venues. Someone once told me that Elvis played here. It's probably apocryphal but I choose to believe it. This journey was teeth-grinding as it was, because it meant missing Chuck Prophet's 'official showcase' at the same time, but Elliott Brood were only doing one show and I wasn't going to miss it.

After that, something calming was required and that was provided once again in the sanctuary of the 18th floor of the Hilton Garden Inn. Tom Brosseau's decision to dispense with all forms of amplification was a blessed change from the rowdiness of the day.

SATURDAY

The best-laid plans ... The idea today was to amble out to the Mean Eyed Cat for the Mojo day party, but no one had anticipated the weather intervening in such a dramatic way. Overnight, the temperature had dropped by forty degrees fahrenheit! In the morning, there was sleet in the air. All day, the whole of Austin was remarkably quiet, the queues non-existent and the few brave souls around the place were wrapped in blankets and cagoules. Most of us, of course, had no such gear with us. I ended up buying three band tee-shirts during the course of the day and wearing all of them on top of the two I started out with. Thank goodness for the sanctuary of the Six Shooter House, where we had been kindly invited to spend the morning but ended up spending hours, because everyone there was so convivial, the endless Margaritas and quiches so irresistible and the music so wonderful (they set up a studio in the cellar and do impromptu live recordings).

Luckily, the house was a stone's throw from Home Slice Pizza, a mine of cool music, and the inimitable Yard Dog Gallery, where we caught Jon Langford, followed by yet another Chuck Prophet show. Goodness knows how any of them managed to play any chords without their digits falling off.

At this stage I had planned to see Athlete, but had been saddened the day before to see a snatch of them reduced to an uninspiring acoustic duo. When their first album came out, I'd have bet on them being a world-beating band, but it's been pretty much downhill from there. So it was off for a final visit to the Red Eyed Fly (this time with no problem about getting in, for obvious reasons) to listen to a few new songs from Ben Weaver. When I shook his hand it literally felt like a block of ice, so goodness knows how he managed to play the banjo. Wrapped up in his hoodie, he had the air of a benevolent monk.

Now this is pretty shaming, but at this stage, I chickened out. On my list of unwatched bands for Sunday evening, I find Gemma Ray, Drums, Ian McLagan, Grant Hart and Swervedriver, but not only was the cold unbearable, but I was back into 'panic about waking up' mode. What if I don't hear the alarm clock? What if the taxi driver doesn't hear his / her alarm clock? Oh god, how will I ever get home (etc, etc)? But the next day, remembering previous years when I have partied till 2 am on the last night and then had to get a morning flight feeling completely shit … well, I didn't regret it.

And the best thing about the return flights? Waving goodbye to my bag at Austin Bergstrom airport and seeing it pop out in Southampton. How is that possible? It always seems like some kind of miracle, to be repeated next March (of course).

VENUE FOCUS: 18TH FLOOR OF THE HILTON GARDEN INN

It is difficult, but it is just possible to escape the mayhem of the average SXSW showcase and find a hidden oasis of tranquility. In stark contrast to the sticky, sweaty vibe of most venues, if you can negotiate your way to the 18th floor of the Hilton Garden Inn, you'll find a sophisticated and luxurious environment in which to enjoy some acoustic music. It's not easy to find, as you have to negotiate various corridors and locate the appropriate elevator, but as you step out into the air-conditioned room, complete with comfy seats and sofas, you are entering a different world. The calibre of the artists is no less strong than elsewhere, simply a lot less loud. I've even been known to go there when I've never heard of who is playing, merely to gain respite for an hour or so. If you're lucky, you can stumble on something quite exciting on the 18th floor. Freedy Johnson and Nils Frahm were memorable, but the standout was an early performance by Kate Stables, before This Is The Kit had been created. Solo with a banjo, she kept the sparse crowd enchanted. Sparse, yes, because very few people actually discover this place, where surprisingly, the drinks are no more expensive than in any of the downtown dive bars. This isn't the only quiet, air-conditioned room on the showcase circuit. There is one more which is on the ground floor of the Driskill hotel on 6th Street and it's known as Steven F's Bar, but somehow that one is lacking in character by comparison.

BANDS SEEN IN 2010

Admiral Radley
Asteroids Galaxy Tour
Band Of Horses
The Beauties
The Besnard Lakes
Sarah Borges & The Broken Singles
Boxer Rebellion
Tom Brosseau
Centro-matic
The Coal Porters
The Deadstring Brothers
Luke Doucet
Drive By Truckers
Elliott Brood
Hot Panda
Jon Langford
The Low Anthem
Mark Mallman & Ruby Isle
Melissa McClelland

Midlake
Nive Nielsen
Chuck Prophet & The Mission Express
Christopher Rees
Justin Rutledge
Shearwater
Spoon
Ben Weaver
You Say Party! We Say Die!

YEAR 9: 2011 / MARCH 15 - 19

Distilled from reviews in the Hampshire Chronicle,
Record Collector and Caught In The Act.

WEDNESDAY

Wednesday afternoon presented an opportunity to have a listen to the much-vaunted Vaccines. This was the first of ten shows in three days for them, and their Home Counties take on the Ramones went down a storm. Unfortunately, their white skinny jeans bring to mind Razorlight, and it's worth remembering that they, too, were a SXSW 'buzz band' just a few years ago. At the moment there's certainly more style than substance in the Vaccines, but it's early days.

There was a San Francisco showcase going on round the corner in the Red Eyed Fly, which was a good opportunity to check out the excellent Spinto Band, the happening Dodos and wait in vain for Mark Eitzel, the reason I was actually there. There was no explanation for a completely different (and useless) band going on when he was due, while Mark sat and watched on in bemusement. This encounter would have to wait.

There followed a failed attempt to get into Stubb's to see James Blake (just out of curiosity really). It's a shame that it's almost impossible to get into the big shows if you aren't willing to queue for hours and forego everything else. I wasn't willing, not even for Foo Fighters or (gulp) Duran Duran, so it was off to the Black and Tan Bar for the aural smash and grab raid that is Edmonton's Hot

Panda. Not a million miles from Barry Adamson-era XTC, they are young, quirky and pure fun.

Sixth Street was hotting up and a couple of wildly crushed shows followed in quick succession. I've always loved The Dears, and a gremlin-bedevilled Murray Lightburn was on fire as he celebrated his fortieth birthday in the familiar prog rock maelstrom. Just next door, on a stage she obviously considered a little small for her, was Ellie Goulding, of whom massive posters and projections were featured all over town. It's always kind of exciting to see a big star in a place the size of a postage stamp, but it's hard to see quite what's special about her. She's like Kylie with a worse hairstyle.

After all that craziness, calm needed to be restored, and that was provided by the beautifully soothing music of Vetiver in St David's Church. So soothing, in fact, that I dropped off in the pews.

THURSDAY

Thursday started in a way that is very typical of SXSW. Being intrigued to see a band called Yuck (simply because they are called Yuck), I walked many miles and then stood in an immobile queue for an hour while, presumably, the band played inside. Then it was a four-mile hike to the opposite end of town to my next scheduled show, but it was worth the sore feet. She Keeps Bees is a fantastic soulful power duo like a reversed-out White Stripes. In their element in the quaint vinyl treasure trove of record store End Of An Ear, the only unfortunate thing for them is the current prevalence of bands with Bees in their names. A delicious (free) beer in the sunny courtyard next door and it was time for a truly wonderful band from Portland called Dolorean. Yearning songs and an understated presence made for a beautiful atmosphere.

Not far away is one of the best 'secret' SXSW daytime venues, Home Slice Pizza. As the sun blazed down, the running order in cheerful disarray, we grooved to the lilting melodies of Great Lake Swimmers and simply swooned as Mark Eitzel and Marc Capelle ran through some American Music Club classics, minus poor Vudi, who was stuck in traffic and arrived (cool as a cucumber of course) just as they finished.

The Strokes were playing at Lady Bird Lake and a mini-riot was breaking out as I arrived, with the barricades being breached. Despite the band being mere dots on the horizon and the sound that of a distant tannoy, their snappy simplicity and style still shone through. Now, one has to suffer for one's pleasure and I have particularly suffered over the years at Cedar Street Courtyard in an effort to get close to much-admired bands. My weakness for The Bangles meant I was willing to endure the torture of standing though categorically two of the worst support bands in world history to be in the front row. Was it worth it? It surely was, as the Bangles blasted through a greatest hits set, still looking like teenagers although they must be approaching fifty. Eternal Flame was positively tear-inducing and they climaxed with an inspired segue of Walk Like An Egyptian and The Who's Magic Bus.

FRIDAY

Friday began in a similarly frustrating way as Thursday. My old pal Julian Dawson was due to read from his new book on the life of Nicky Hopkins at Waterloo Records but was running late. Outside, the Dum Dum Girls were performing (great, by the way), so I had to leave before Julian started, as I had a date at the Yard Dog Gallery on South Congress, scene of some of the best boozy day parties. Strutting her stuff was Exene Cervenka (previously of the band X), her punk attitude being enthusiastically applied to her clever, melodic songs, with vocal support from Cindy Wassermann of Dead Rock West and some gorgeous psychedelic pedal steel from Maggie Bjorklund. You wouldn't want to tangle with Exene.

In a dramatic change of atmosphere that was to be typical of the day, we found ourselves next in the plushy but almost empty Convention Center ballroom, where the sparky Caitlin Rose was clearly spooked by the formal atmosphere. Great pedal steel here too, from Spencer Cullum Jr, and fabulous Steve Cropper style guitar from the impossibly youthful Jeremy Fetzer.

It was back to the most primeval down and dirty rock and roll imaginable as we joined the mischievous Jesse Malin in the tiny Aquarium Bar on Sixth. Jesse and his St Mark's Social duly laid waste to the place, with Jesse prancing along the bar, then getting everyone to lie on the floor before finishing with a singalong Instant Karma. He's like a naughty New York schoolboy intent on causing trouble, which he certainly does.

A final desperate and unsuccessful attempt to see Yuck later, we ended up with Lucinda Williams in the brand new Moody Theater. She's a country-rock legend and her band consists of the slickest musos in the business, with massively impressive dual lead guitars. Unfortunately, though, with her Dusty Springfield panda eyes and her super-professional but largely immobile stage presence, it was an impressive rather than an emotional experience.

SATURDAY

Saturday was the day of the traditional Mojo barbecue at the Mean Eyed Cat. Because the venue is so far off the beaten track, it tends to be sparsely attended, despite the stellar nature of the line-up. This gives it a real feel of occasion, a genuine privilege to be able to attend. Me, I'm always transfixed by Phil Alexander, Mojo's editor, who not only compères the show but also makes copious notes. It's all I can do to prevent myself from sidling up and trying to squint at his notes, so as to get a sneak preview of the review in the following month's magazine.

Nicely fuelled by Margaritas and quiche from the Six Shooter Records brunch, we experienced an unbelievable sequence of contrasting acts, all of them brilliant in their way: garage punk crossed with Little Richard from the blindingly good Jim Jones Revue, pastoral melodies from Erland and the Carnival, Louisiana swamp-folk from Hurray For The Riff Raff and acoustic storytelling from the beatific Josh T. Pearson, the man with the kind eyes. You haven't lived until you've heard his extraordinary cover of Boney

M's Rivers Of Babylon.

The weekend was completed by some true Americana music. At Antone's, Joe Ely and his ultra-slick band did the trick (we'll draw a veil over headliners Hansen), while at Jax Bar, Eilen Jewell was as charming as ever, sending me home to the cold UK with a warm heart.

VENUE FOCUS: GUERO'S

Another book on this topic would probably have an entire chapter on Austin eateries but this is not something that Paul and I have ever been able to research much, firstly because I'm not really bothered about food, but mainly because we are constantly on the move and seldom have time to pause. Quite early in our visits, we discovered the place where we were fated to spend many hours. Indeed, we've been known to create gaps in our schedule specifically in order to go there. In the busy and bohemian South Congress area, not far from the Continental Club, can be found Guero's, a huge Tex-Mex restaurant with gorgeous food that also has its own venue in the garden. My abilities as a food critic are limited but I would encourage anybody visiting Austin to head straight to Guero's and try out the shrimp enchiladas or the vegan cashew queso, which are sensational. Live music takes place outside all year but cranks up over South By Southwest, mainly concentrating on local musicians such as Ghost Wolves, John Dee Graham and Scrappy Jud Newcombe.

One year we encountered Frank Turner in the garden. Frank attends South By Southwest regularly and, being such a hard-working trouper, plays around ten to fifteen shows over the few days. I have tried and tried to enjoy Frank Turner's music. Everyone I know loves him. He comes from where I live in Hampshire, he's hugely popular around the world, yet somehow I just can't enjoy the style, which we know as 'shouty-strummy-preachy' and, to be honest, can be found in almost any pub on a Saturday night. Plus I'm prejudiced against him because he went to Eton. I'm sorry, but I'm being honest.

On the other hand, I know for a fact that he's a deeply-caring, highly empathetic guy who connects on a visceral level with any audience he encounters. I know that he is one of the few artists who regularly gives back to the music industry at a grassroots level. I'm also aware, since reading his autobiography, that he had to suffer an extremely peculiar and challenging upbringing. I am certain that if we actually met, we would get on like a house on fire on a personal level, but yet ... but yet, I just cannot get over all the shouting and strumming. Predictably, Frank went down a storm with the assembled Texans at Guero's, even though most of them probably had little comprehension of his mainly UK-based political lyrics. It is a measure of how unusual Austin is politically, compared to the rest of Texas, that both Frank Turner and Billy Bragg are hugely popular here.

BANDS SEEN IN 2011

The Bangles
Exene Cervenka
Dodos
Dolorean
The Dum Dum Girls
Mark Eitzel & Marc Capelle
Joe Ely
Erland & The Carnival
Ellie Goulding
Great Lake Swimmers
Hansen
Herman Dune
Hot Panda
Hurray For The Riff Raff
Eilen Jewell
Jitterbug Vipers
The Jim Jones Revue

Murray Lightburn
Jesse Malin & The Saint Mark's Social
Josh T. Pearson
Caitlin Rose
Sea Of Bees
She Keeps Bees
Spinto Band
The Strokes
This Is The Kit
The Vaccines
Vetiver
Lucinda Williams

YEAR 10: 2012 / MARCH 13 - 17

Distilled from reviews in the Hampshire Chronicle,
Record Collector and Caught In The Act.

This year, I'm going to try to give an idea of what it's really like coping with SXSW. You'll probably find the detail wearisome and you'll probably be shocked by some of the music. I have very Catholic tastes. But when I am too old and knackered to do it any more, maybe I'll read this back and wallow in the memories.

Getting up a 4 am to catch the 5 o'clock coach to Heathrow was challenging, but actually there was something rather relaxing about being in town at that quiet time of day. Everybody on the coach was asleep apart from a couple at the back who had a blazing row which lasted the entire journey. What kind of energy must you have to fight at 5 am?

I've never had such a lovely flight. Following the merger of Continental and United, there is over-capacity on transatlantic routes and the plane was less than a quarter full. I lay down across three seats and, after a lovely veggie lunch, used the three blankets and three pillows to create a bed and slept like a lamb for the entire flight.

Actually, I hadn't booked this route at all (via Newark). I'd booked via Houston but received a casual email saying the route had been changed. This meant a very short connection in Newark, so I was hoping for a smooth immigration process. Inevitably, I chose the only queue with an over-zealous officer and a series of people with apparent problems. As the other queues were waved by with a smile, mine stubbornly refused to move. Then came security. The queue I chose was hijacked by a series of people in wheelchairs. In my panic, my natural inclination to give them the consideration they merited was almost overcome with a desire to shout "Get out of the bloody way, can't you see I'm in a hurry?" - but not quite, of course. On the plane, I sat next to a very nice Dutch agent. Unfortunately he had a streaming cough and cold and I had to try to face away from him while still maintaining a conversation. Buggered if I was going to let my SXSW be ruined by a cold.

Paul was waiting at the airport and we headed straight for the Convention Centre to get my badge. As I'd slept so well, there were no jet lag symptoms at all. I was desperate for an enchilada and luckily a suitable emporium was just opposite. The waitress tried to convince us that the obviously chain establishment was owned by her father.

This was the year when something befell me that I think is quite common in transatlantic travel but has never happened to me before or since: My luggage got lost. So as the final cool musician retrieved the last stencilled flight case and disappeared, there I was, watching the empty carousel trundle around and finally grind to a halt. In the morning, we had to head for the nearest Walmart in order for me to purchase a toothbrush, toothpaste, pants, socks and a couple of (actually rather stylish) shirts. On the third morning, my bag suddenly appeared, unannounced, in the hotel foyer, where anyone could have stolen it but luckily no one did.

We headed straight for the 'British Embassy' at a club called Latitude just off Sixth Street. This is where, each year, a succession of usually mediocre and never-to-be-heard-of-again UK bands play, apparently at our expense. "Thank you Austin", they all chant as they announce their long-awaited final numbers. Among those playing this year was 'Charlie from Busted' (honestly).

We know that one of the quirks of my annual visit is that I have to write about bands from my area for the local paper. Frank Turner is the only 'famous' rocker ever to have come from Winchester (apart from Mike Batt, but he doesn't count). You've already read what I think of Frank but it was vital to get a photo of him, so in we went. It turned out to be a good move, because we caught a great band from Wales called Future Of The Left, who were highly political and roared like buffaloes on heat. After that, Frank Turner announced he was going to play his 'hits'. I wasn't aware he had any.

After a nice sleep in the Homestead Suite which was home for the week, it was time to make some of the awful decisions that have to be made every few minutes at SXSW. Daytime activities on the Radio Day Stage of the Convention Center have become much more exciting than they used to be, and here you can catch many of the 'buzz bands' in plush surroundings, complete with huge, dreamy bean bags. Thus it was that we were able to see three acts in just over an hour: Michael Kiwanuka (making his US debut and being very pleasantly soulful), the lovely Whitehorse, (Luke Doucet and Melissa McClelland demonstrating their new-found technological expertise in the adjacent Brush Square) and then back to the Day Stage for the much-anticipated Alabama Shakes. They fit the bill for the Adele audience perfectly and it's not unrealistic to imagine similar success for them.

Now here's an odd thing. As well as the clashes, there are moments when there's nothing to do. Such was the case next, so we wandered over to the South Congress area. This is where the cool art galleries and eateries are, plus the back yards where band after band can be found playing, so there's always some music to catch. After another round of shrimp enchiladas (I could have them for breakfast, lunch and tea for the rest of my life), plus some happy hour beers (Dos Equis, two dollars a bottle), we hung around for some great music featuring Scrappy Jud Newcombe and an unidentified vocalist who looked as if he were about to die but sang like an angel. Then, via the already burgeoning mayhem of Sixth, we caught Jeff Klein's My Jerusalem at Trinity Hall.

I'd heard of Dry The River (or maybe it was one of the many other bands which have River in their name), so off we went to the Red Eyed Fly. Well, I hadn't done my research, because they weren't American but British. They were weird, but not in a good way. There was something disconcerting about the giant tattooed bassist leaping on and off the drum riser and then introducing the next song in a fey Home Counties accent entirely at odds with the image. I'd expected something authentic, which this certainly wasn't. On the 18th Floor of the Hilton, Freedy Johnson was lovely at midnight, playing Cruel To Be Kind on a ukelele. One of the highlights of the week actually, and how nice to relax on a comfy seat.

That day's final madness was the misguided idea Paul had that a band featuring Wayne Coyne's nephew from Oklahoma must signal a secret show from the Flaming Lips. It didn't, but they were fun nonetheless. Not enough fun to prevent us from heading for the hotel though.

Thursday was going to be Springsteen day. Attendance at his show was to be decided by lottery. So far so good, but the winners were to be notified by email. My phone wasn't so technically adept, so I was reduced to asking people if I could borrow their iPhones to check. I never heard anything, but soon was cursing my stupidity.

No one was supposed to know where the concert would take place, but I should have spotted it. I'd noted down The Low Anthem, one of my favourite bands, as a show to go to at the Moody Theater. Straight after was Alejandro Escovedo, followed by nothing. As Alejandro and Springsteen share a manager, it was bloody obvious what was going to happen - and I failed to realize. Pathetic.

Time waits for no one, and particularly when it's a question of getting into the Cedar Street Courtyard. The showcase I had spotted showed an afternoon sequence, in this order, of Band Of Skulls, Kaiser Chiefs and Keane. Few things are as thrilling as being very close to a huge band, even if they aren't necessarily your favourites. To achieve this, you have to go several hours early and tolerate the innumerable supports, because obviously a show such as this would be ridiculously over-subscribed.

Well, it's very annoying for someone like me, who prefers things to be as they should. Admission to the showcase was supposed to be only for those who have RSVPd in advance and received an acknowledgement, a procedure which I had dutifully followed weeks before. In the event, what actually happens is that they simply randomly let everyone in regardless until it's full. Luckily I knew this was likely to happen, which was why we arrived two hours in advance.

Duly installed dangerously in front of the speakers, we settled down for the afternoon, surrounded by lots of affable and mildly intoxicated new friends. The first band were awful Simple Minds clones, the second were certifiably insane and the third was Band Of Skulls. They have deservedly gone mega in the States since last year and I genuinely felt proud to come from (near) Southampton. Plus they are all very photogenic, by which I mean that photos come out showing them as they actually are, rather than as gurning gargoyles. Next up: Kaiser Chiefs, loads of fun, swaggeringly confident and essentially going through the motions, but still a thrill greater than you'd get from seeing them in a stadium. Keane were quite unable to follow them. I'm sorry, but you don't come to Austin without a guitar.

I'd been recommended The War On Drugs, so after sitting on the kerb eating a huge lukewarm chunk of pizza, I headed to the Mohawk Patio early, fearful of crowds. I ended up crushed against the front of the stage, far too close to the speakers. In fact, my ears are still ringing a week later. It meant that the sound was so distorted that I couldn't work out whether I actually liked them or not. I'll give them another go.

What followed was an unexpected highlight. Billed at the Hilton (ground floor) was 'Special Guest (Framlingham, UK)'. This could, of course, only mean Ed Sheeran, so I got there early, assuming it would be rammed, with queues round the block. Ed was doing several other shows during the week, all in much bigger venues. But that was without reckoning on the difference of tastes between the UK and the US, nor the way that careers develop at different rates in different countries. Basically, the place was half empty, and it was only a small hotel conference room anyway, laid out, cabaret style, with tables, chairs and candles. At first I blundered straight into Ed's dressing room and had to beat a hasty retreat. He was applying ointment to a bloodstained forearm, recovering from an afternoon encounter with a brutal tattooist. Then (I'd had a couple of drinks), I marched straight to the front and sat down at a table by the stage. This gave a good vantage point, firstly for the excellent Marcus Foster, then for Ed himself.

Bloody hell, he's good. I am instinctively prejudiced against anything commercially successful, particularly if bound up with Brit Awards and the like. Also, the 'solo bloke with acoustic guitar and loop pedals' concept is so hackneyed. Well, not this time. He's ridiculously talented as a songwriter, uses the gizmos brilliantly and brought the house down with his rapping. At the end (he always does this but I'd forgotten), he clambered on top of my very table and did a couple of unamplified songs. He was wearing very baggy shorts and it was tempting to point my camera up them. I resisted.

There is photographic evidence of me reclining at a table with Ed Sheeran on top of it, inches away from me. In the photo, I appear to be fast asleep. I most certainly was not, but I had not reckoned with the huge hatred that Ed would engender among knowledgeable music buffs, who would scream with laughter if I admitted to liking him. Therefore, I have since then happily let people believe I was actually asleep, in order to retain my street credibility.

By the end of the long walk home, I was knackered enough to cancel morning appointments and opt to sleep instead. Just as well, since it would be another long day. It started with the beginning of a ridiculous but magical Chuck Prophet odyssey. He was playing at the excellent Ginger Man Pub, not even listed as a venue, but centrally placed and with a great patio and stage. Here I found a nest of UK promoters, all discussing the Springsteen show. Apparently it had been possible just to walk in there unchallenged. There'd even been empty seats. People were saying it hadn't been anything special - phew. In fact, a couple of songs into Chuck's set, all the talk was about Chuck being significantly more exciting. Basically, you've never seen a better rock act. His band is astounding and the new songs from the Temple Beautiful album uniformly appealing. And Chuck's guitar shredding is beyond belief. So when Peter Buck stepped up and joined in the You Did finale, it was more that anyone could ever have hoped for on a Friday lunchtime.

Time for a bit of comfort at the Day Stage. The target was Blitzen Trapper but I arrived in time for the end of Ben Kweller's set. This guy was being hyped all over the place, on billboards, buses and taxis, but it was hard to see why. Blitzen Trapper were much more interesting.

Next was a long trek to a venue called Lustre Pearl. On the way, we saw a bleeding guy who'd been knocked off his bike. The show was organized by the same magazine as the previous day's Cedar Street showcase, so needless to say, the same chaotic admission procedure reigned and my RSVP was cheerfully ignored, indeed laughed at. Eventually we saw snatches of Deerhoof (good) and The Drums (Strokes clones) but the call of hunger was irresistible and a visit to a nearby chain burger joint reinforced what we really already knew: chain burger joints are to be avoided.

Then I did something silly. Keen to see M. Ward, I set off for a small venue called Frank. Wandering past a quarter mile queue, I vaguely wondered who was causing it, until I got to the venue and realized it was the front of the queue. Bloody stupid, of course I should have realized M. Ward was far too big for a little venue and that I should have gone along hours earlier. Nevertheless, I joined the line but it didn't move at all and eventually we were informed that it was 'one out, one in'. So that'll mean getting in some time next week then.

But there was an alternative. Over at Joe's on South Congress, Alejandro Escovedo's Orchestra was about to start playing. It was a hell of a long walk, so the time had come to try out the ubiquitous bike rickshaws. I was a little surprised that a clutch of them declined to take me when I said where I wanted to go. "No thanks man, that's up a hill", was the response. Eventually one agreed to do it for twenty dollars. It was actually a bit hair-raising. Austin prides itself on its eco-friendliness, but it hasn't really got its transport act properly together. Taxis are not to be found in the centre during SXSW because gridlock reigns and they'd never get anywhere. The status of the rickshaws seems vague. As we trundled along the road, motorists charged dangerously by, honking at us to get out of the way. So then we took to the sidewalk, whereupon we were quite rightly shouted at by angry pedestrians. On a couple of occasions I had to dismount because we couldn't get through gaps left by parked cars. Anyway we eventually got to Joe's, where a huge crowd was being entertained by the orchestra. There were no 'special guests' but a great version of Rock The Casbah.

It was back to the mayhem of Sixth for a moment, where I was tapped on the shoulder and turned to find the son of a friend of mine from Cornwall. That's crazy! As was Grant Hart, who I was interested to see because Bob Mould was in town performing Copper Blue but I couldn't work out where. Hart was shambling alone in front of a sparse audience and appeared to have no teeth. I lasted thirty seconds.

Shearwater was strange too. They've suddenly turned into a rock band, losing two of their most important members (drummer Thor and bassist Kim Burke) and thus losing much of their original appeal. I was cheered up by bumping into my friend Al James from Dolorean but shocked to find the beers at Red Seven cost six dollars each. Cheek!

Saturday started with something very pleasant, a secret show from Laura Gibson and band in her hotel room, complete with a delicious breakfast courtesy of her record company. Things like that at SXSW are so special. But the rest of the day was to be designated as Chuck Prophet Day. Paul had decided he wanted to follow Chuck round Austin because he was so bloody good. Paul had a car, I was feeling less inclined to rush around checking out other artists and basically, the idea was irresistible. So there we were at Jovita's, drinking beer at 1 pm (it feels deliciously decadent) and having our brains blown out by the storming Mission Express. Someone videoed lots of this show; try putting 'Chuck Prophet, Jovitas' into You Tube. The ear-to-ear grins sported by the entire band tell you everything.

After a few minutes of the Waco Brothers it was off to the Yard Dog Gallery courtyard for the next Chuck instalment. This was enlivened by two power cuts, which hardly seemed to matter, because the audience just kept on singing until it was sorted out. Noticing that Ian McLagan would be playing at the Yard Dog later, we zipped over to Maria's Taco Express, where the impeccably dapper Alejandro Escovedo was presiding over his annual taco party and a huge array of bands of wildly differing style and quality. Back at Yard Dog, the Mekons' Jon Langford and the indefatigable Ian McLagan were finishing off the day in style. Expat Brits both, they sum up the joy of being a musician in this particular town. Mac observed that he had now lived in the US as long as he had lived in London. He also suggested visiting Austin outside of SXSW, when there is still plenty of music to choose from.

Getting towards the end now, I had a hankering to check out hotly-tipped new Scottish band Django Django, and it was worth it. Despite being at the oddly-shaped and very uncomfortable Latitude club, they impressed with their stoned synths and raging percussion. Plus their bassist was a dead ringer for Thomas Dolby (who was also in town somewhere).

My plan was to finish off the week with a nice quiet dose of Hurray For The Riff Raff, but it turned out they had actually been on at 12.30 lunchtime rather than midnight, so the trip had been fruitless. The only solution was another rickshaw (and another complaint about pedalling uphill) back to the Continental Club for a final helping of Chuck, preceded by a frighteningly loud Jon Dee Graham and Freedy Johnson, quite different from the acoustic version previously encountered. I still don't know if it's true that Elvis once played at the Continental, but it certainly feels as if the spirit of rock and roll is embedded in its walls.

And so to bed and a completely uneventful trip home. Next year is already booked.

VENUE FOCUS: JOVITA'S

I only went to Jovita's twice but its story is quite something. Yet another Tex-Mex restaurant doubling up as a music venue, it played host to some big hitters. As well as a memorable Chuck Prophet show, I also experienced Graham Parker backed by The Figgs. The venue had a strong reputation for a high quality sound system and for paying its bands well. But there was a hidden secret.

On June 22, 2012, news broke that Jovita's had been raided and shut down as a heroin distribution hub. A year-long investigation by the FBI concluded that the owner Amando Pardo, arrested with 14 of his associates, had served three prison sentences in the 70s and 80s, including two for murder.

Seen as a responsible community leader, it turned out that Pardo was selling up to 6 thousand dollars' worth of heroin a day from Jovita's. Sometimes, the restaurant was used to cut and package the heroin in balloons, but Pardo had given Austin musicians a stage to play on and good payments. Pardo died of liver cancer in January 2013 at age 64, a month before the trial, proclaiming his innocence to the end.

BANDS SEEN IN 2012

Alabama Shakes
Band Of Skulls
Blitzen Trapper
Jimmy Cliff
Deerhoof
Django Django
Luke Doucet
The Drums
Dry The River
Alejandro Escovedo's Orchestra

Marcus Foster
Future Of The Left
Laura Gibson
Jon Dee Graham
Grant Hart
Freedy Johnson
Kaiser Chiefs
Keane
Michael Kiwanuka
Ian McLagan & Jon Langford
My Jerusalem
Scrappy Jud Newcombe
Chuck Prophet & The Mission Express
Shearwater
Ed Sheeran
Frank Turner
The Waco Brothers
The War On Drugs
Whitehorse

YEAR 11: 2013 / MARCH 12 - 16

Distilled from reviews in the Hampshire Chronicle,
Record Collector and Caught In The Act.

This is going to read like a 'Dear Diary' piece, but I can't think of any other approach. This is what we did, and this is what we saw.

Wednesday kicked off with new Loose signing Jonny Fritz at a far-flung venue called Weather Up, getting to which started work on the blisters that would characterise the week. The genial Fritz was slightly upstaged by an extraordinarily off-the-wall performance from John McCauley, looking wasted but sounding sublime, as, alone with an electric guitar, he gave us enticing previews of what is clearly shaping up to be a fantastic new Deer Tick album.

There was blistering sunshine at this expertly-curated showcase sponsored by a shirt manufacturer. Along with Hotel Vegas, Weather Up is one of a number of nice venues east of Highway 35, where a more laid-back vibe is in evidence than on the increasingly frantic and commercialised Sixth Street area for which Austin is famous. All the artists seemed to know each other and there was much hilarity as John McCauley launched into a drug-related confessional monologue. Looking on with interest was Taylor Goldsmith of Dawes, who was standing immediately next to me but who induced such a bout of starstruck-dom that I didn't dare say a word to him. I would have had so much to ask, we made eye contact on several occasions but nothing came of it. To this day, I regret not doing a bit of fawning, but it's too late now.

At the plushy Convention Centre a Swiss girl band called - yes - Boy were doing a passable First Aid Kit impression. I was all set to dislike Jake Bugg, especially as he looks as if he is yet to sit his GCSEs, but actually he was unaffected by the environment, making no attempt to ingratiate himself other than with his good voice and nifty songs. A good guy with a strong future.

Back to Weather Up for a beautiful set from the Milk Carton Kids, gossamer-light harmonies and self-deprecating humour abounding. You'd never think they hailed from Los Angeles, but they do, as do the magnificent Dawes, who followed. This was just the third of their twelve - count 'em - SXSW performances, but they sounded sublime, playing to a hundred or so sun-kissed souls and presenting a load of new songs which bear their trade mark of being instantly accessible.

Now it was time to prepare for being unable to get in to Stubb's for Nick Cave, but no, the queue moved swiftly and I was able to get in the front row, ready to get my head blown off. A Nick Cave performance is more a triumph of theatricality than a traditional rock show but deeply affecting nonetheless, swaggering with confidence. After that, it was a bit of a comedown to be confronted with the sub-Eltonisms of Tom Odell, including a horrifically misjudged attempt at Honky Tonk Women. The evening finished at the comfortable Stephen F's Bar, not really designed for music but a nice place for Welsh roots artist Christopher Rees. After that, it was tempting to go and see Dawes again at the Moody Theater, but that would have felt like stalking, and tiredness triumphed.

Thursday would be a long haul, but worth it. At the cosy Ginger Man venue, the Waterboys' Mike Scott was kicking the day off with some traditional folk. At the Paste stage, Hurray For The Riff Raff were entertaining a big crowd, but I was on a mission to find Allah-Las, which entailed walking agonizing miles to an amiable dump called the Scoot Inn, situated in a wasteland and doubling as the venue for a diverting skateboard competition. Squeezed in among various unidentified metal bands, the dapper Allah-Las took me back to my teens. Their vocals and stage moves were pure Herman's Hermits. Twee, sure, but I loved every moment.

Back in the Convention Center, Hiss Golden Messenger was flu-ridden and fresh off a plane, so it would be unfair to judge him on his allotted twenty minutes. So it was off to the Chuggin' Monkey, a typical Sixth Street dive, for Peter Bruntnell and band, on sparkling form presenting their new Retrospective compilation. Then on to Mellow Johnny's Bike Shop (one of the more inimitable SXSW venues, famously owned by Lance Armstrong and not at all suitable for music) for the much-anticipated reunion of the True Believers, with Alejandro Escovedo and Jon Dee Graham. They rocked out with aplomb but the volume was so ludicrously excessive that I was lured by the siren call of some shrimp fajitas. Well, you gotta eat some time.

A short queuing process allowed access to Austin's famous blues cavern, Antone's, for a typically well-judged half-hour of Richard Thompson and his hot electric band, opening with a blistering Tear Stained Letter which was one of the week's highlights. Sadly, it was followed by a very low lowlight. A high-risk queuing strategy surprisingly allowed us admission to the small-scale Flaming Lips show at the Belmont (they would do the full production extravaganza the next night at Auditorium Shores). Things were running very late, which meant that we were exposed to the bland horror of an entire set by Alt-J. Insipid, soulless and generally useless, they nearly sent everyone to sleep with their warbles and bleeps. Considering Depeche Mode were in town, they should have hung their heads in shame.

Even the Flaming Lips were a let-down, and I never thought I'd say that. They'd decided to forsake all their visuals and perform the whole of Yoshimi vs The Pink Robots, but it didn't really work. The augmented band was strangely hesitant and disjointed, and with little to catch the attention, it sort of fizzled out.

On Friday, there was the most ridiculously high quality showcase going on at Waterloo Records, with the likes of Frightened Rabbit,

Richard Thompson, Emmylou Harris and (gulp) Alt-J, but I was desperate not to miss John Murry, so determinedly headed to the far-flung Hole In The Wall to experience him playing just four songs to a small but rapt audience. This led on (after some amiable psychedelia from the Besnard Lakes at Ginger Man) to one of those endearingly unique SXSW experiences, as John Murry agreed to spend the day with us. Surreal wasn't the word, as we found ourselves miles outside town in a fabulous, classic roadhouse called the Sahara Lounge. It was Happy Hour and the venue's speciality was an unspecified and evil concoction called Devil's Piss. Here, Peter Bruntnell and band were playing pool but no one else was present. If it hadn't been for me, John Murry and Paul, they would have been playing to their tour manager and the sound engineer. This, I hasten to say, didn't indicate any lack of popularity, simply that it was in the middle of nowhere and no one knew about it. The Bruntnell band (featuring Dave Little on storming guitar) cheerfully blasted through Pete's greatest hits, doubtless fuelled by the Devil's Piss.

Canada House this year was situated at Friends, in the full-on bedlam of Sixth Street. Here, Whitehorse (Luke Doucet and Melissa McClelland) proved themselves masters of the mountain of technology they've acquired and now sound, as a duo, more like a six-piece band. The energy is breathtaking.

At Red River, a far from sold-out Stubb's played host to Cold War Kids who were deservedly received with deafening silence, and to the Specials, who caused frantic skanking with an unashamedly hit-laden set. They were going through the motions in the most pleasant way, seemingly sponsored by Grecian 2000.

Saturday was the day in which you could have seen, in true crazily eclectic SXSW fashion, the Zombies, Eric Burdon, Charlotte Church or Prince (we didn't). Arguably more fun, and certainly more intimate, was the Yard Dog Gallery (it's a blistering suntrap), where the Minus Five featured both Scott McCaughey and the legendary Clem Burke. After that, Austin's lucky mascot, Ian McLagan, presented a bunch of new songs, plus of course the classic You're So Rude.

Then it was on to the Broken Spoke, where line dancing is the norm. Country star Laura Cantrell and the gimmicky Pokey Lafarge were both put firmly in the shade by the cheerful Caitlin Rose - small of stature but big of lung - and her hot band. Not far away, Alejandro Escovedo's day party was taking place at Maria's. As we listened to the Mastersons, I drank a couple of exquisite Margaritas, which had unfortunate consequences. Emboldened by the Tequila and finding I had my credit card in my pocket, I proceeded to enter Allen's Boot Store and buy some unsuitable Western shirts that I couldn't afford. Don't ask. I still have them in my wardrobe but wouldn't dream of wearing them.

At Joe's, Dawes were concluding their (almost) final show. With immense courage, they first proved they can stretch out and improvise, then finished with a quiet, slow and brand new song, earning an encore, normally unheard of at SXSW. An hour later, they unexpectedly popped up yet again at the Moody Theater as guest backing band for one song with John Fogerty, whose super slick, over-frantic approach to the Creedence legacy is almost parodic in its overkill. He really didn't need the three extra rhythm guitarists (one of them his son) to back him as he galloped round the stage like Benny Hill.

But as we say every year, "It was the best SXSW ever"!

VENUE FOCUS: THE BROKEN SPOKE

One thing any long-standing inhabitant of Austin will tell you is that "things ain't what they used to be". As the city has expanded very rapidly with incoming tech companies and a booming economy, the 'music capital of the US' accolade has been threatened by other cities such as Nashville. Because many of Austin's venues have been knocked down and turned into office blocks or condos, a once thriving honky-tonk scene is now down to a handful of venues, the most famous of which is the Broken Spoke. You can see the problem as soon as you arrive and try to find somewhere to park.

All around are high-rise buildings with the venue itself miraculously still unscathed in the middle of them. It's frequented by regulars throughout the year and music events continue during SXSW, often under the banner of Twangfest and focusing very much on country rock. The normal clientèle just turns up as usual. They don't seem particularly resentful at some of the more rocky and challenging acts that suddenly invade their space, because they are so obsessed with two-step dancing that they are willing and able to dance through anything, largely ignoring genre or suitability. It's a pretty grotty place, featuring a front bar that has bands playing on the floor by the front door and a scruffy back room with a roomy stage. My abiding memory is of Chuck Prophet striding on stage and declaring, "It's great to be back at the Broken Spoke. If these walls could speak they would say 'clean me, it's f****** dirty in here!'" and indeed, cleanliness is not one of the main features. Yes, the two-steppers continued all the way through Chuck's rocking set.

The most successful You Tube video I've ever filmed in Austin was taken here during the early days of the rise of Sturgill Simpson (the video is currently on 105K views). Completely oblivious to his challenging lyrical content, his left of centre political views and his fantastically inventive rock lead guitarist, the dancers never let up for a second. This activity does make negotiating the route to the toilets quite hazardous, as the dancers tend to swing their arms around a lot. I've never actually seen any evidence of it but I do imagine that it would be inadvisable to bump into anybody on the dance floor. Stetsons and macho poses are very much de rigeur. It's the only place in Austin where I do feel mildly nervous. Maybe that dates back to the occasion when, while queuing for the bar, I turned around and my rucksack inadvertently brushed the back of the lady standing in front of me. She whirled round and accused me of touching her inappropriately. My very British, mild-mannered protestations that nothing could have been further from the truth didn't go down well as she warned me in no uncertain terms that her boyfriend was on the way there and that he carried a gun. Discretion being the better part of valour, I headed for the exit pronto. Nonetheless, the Broken

Spoke is the epitome of non-corporate, genuine Austin music and it fills me with affection.

BANDS SEEN 2013

Allah-Las
Alt J
Boy
Peter Bruntnell
Jake Bugg
Laura Cantrell
Nick Cave
Cold War Kids
Dawes
Steve Earle
The Flaming Lips
John Fogerty
Jonny Fritz
Hiss Golden Messenger
Hurray For The Riff Raff
Pokey LaFarge
The Mastersons
John McCauley
Ian McLagan & The Bump Band
The Milk Carton Kids
The Minus 5
John Murry
Tom Odell
Christopher Rees
Caitlin Rose
Mike Scott
The Specials
Richard Thompson
The True Believers

YEAR 12: 2014 / MARCH 11 - 15

2014 was my first year aided by a direct flight to Austin, started that year by British Airways and helped by the rising profile of the city in tech matters, as well as PGA golf and Formula 1 motor racing.

It was also a landmark year for the ethos of SXSW music, because it ended in tragedy. At 12.30 am on March 13, punters were queuing outside the Mohawk venue to see Tyler the Creator when a man called Rashad Owens ploughed his car into the crowds at 55 mph, near the intersection of East 10th and Red River. Extraordinarily, Owens was an aspiring rapper, in town to perform at a nightclub, when the police tried to pull him over for driving without his headlights on. Owens drove away through a gas station and the wrong way down a one-way street, before crashing through traffic barricades and speeding north on Red River, where he killed four people and injured many others by driving into the crowds. Owens was eventually sentenced to life imprisonment for murder, but the knock-on effects were felt for years to come, as the music festival notably became a lower-key and less crowded affair. I don't know if that was a specific policy by the organisers, but I myself had been becoming increasingly worried about overcrowding and the potential for some kind of unpleasant incident. Of course, never could I have anticipated such an appalling event, but it certainly resonated down the years.

Distilled from reviews in the Hampshire Chronicle,
Record Collector and Caught In The Act.

Everything started well, because the new direct flight means you can arrive not exhausted and head straight out on the Tuesday (each year the music festival seems to start earlier). We caught Kelley Stoltz at Bar 96 (it had been less than a week since we saw him in the UK), and by the time we'd sorted out the badges, it was time for bed, in an attempt to be fresh in the morning. This was foiled by the hotel turning out to be next to a liquor store.

Daylight revealed that on the other side of the hotel was a Mexican breakfast joint, so you can take it for granted that every morning consisted of a long lie-in followed by a blow-out of huevos rancheros and such. I won't mention food again.

A bus into town (you can ride the buses all day for two dollars) took us to Mellow Johnny's Bike Shop, where I promptly bought a branded cap. I didn't really want to advertise Lance Armstrong but forgetting to bring my hat was a poor policy for confronting the Texas climate. Hurray For The Riff Raff were playing here. I was interested to see the effect of their signing to the Alabama Shakes' label ATO. Well, there are no musical changes but an almost complete line-up change, with only Alynda Lee Segarra and Yosi Pearlstein remaining. Then it was on to the lovely suntrap that is the Ginger Man Pub for Wilco members The Autumn Defense, sounding less like Wilco and more like Crowded House, which was just fine. It then took a while to find Capital Cruises, the take-off point for a riverboat ride starring, again, the Kelley Stoltz Band. It's been said before, these guys really know how to have fun. They duly warmed the cockles (it was bloody freezing) and we managed to drink the boat dry. By the end, all they had left was vodka and water. Staggering into nearby Threadgill's, we briefly encountered Austin stalwart James McMurtry and friends.

Paul then inexplicably wanted to see Spandau Ballet (apparently they were great) so I slipped into the ever-intimate Cedar Street Courtyard for the Felice Brothers. They can occasionally be a bit flaky, but not today. They tore the place up. But now the infuriating side of SXSW kicked in. I wanted to see young UK singer Chloë Howl at Latitude. This rather unpleasant venue was, as usual, the headquarters of 'British Music' for the week, i.e. packed with UK music biz types (anyone ever read Kill Your Friends?). The bands think the Texans love them, but actually no Texans are there. Anyway, I'd heard a rumour that Chloë had failed to get a work permit but thought I'd risk it anyway. What a disaster. She was replaced by one of the most ghastly pretentious loads of tosh it has ever been my misfortune to experience. High As A Kite, they were called. Droning and warbling and groaning under the weight of their mountains of expensive equipment, their stodgy music made me almost lose the will to live. I was in a bad mood, I can tell you, and it soon got worse as I fought my way through the crowds of Sixth Street and headed for Stubb's, where St. Vincent was similarly pompous and embarrassingly over the top. She used to be quite good, now she's a poor person's Lady Gaga. Oh well, better hang on for Damon Albarn. No chance. After forty minutes of watching crew set up and check gear, I had to head off to the Flamingo Cantina where Angelo Moore was due to play (members of Chuck Prophet's band were in there, so it could have been interesting). But they, too, were running very late. There were loads of people (too many) in the band, plus a bloody theramin (hate those things). As the clock ticked towards an hour after they were due to start, I gave up. That had made over ninety minutes wasted listening to sound checks. It was a shit end to the first day.

You'd think I'd learn, but I never seem to. For months, I have been keen to see London Grammar, since a friend of mine told me about them last Autumn. I was slightly put off them on learning that they were managed by Jazz Summers, whose terrible (obviously dictated) autobiography I had just finished, but still … Filter magazine organises superb showcases at the Cedar Street Courtyard, a perfect place to see them, as they were one of this year's 'buzz' bands and normally playing much bigger venues. I'd gone through the complicated advance rigmarole of RSVPing for this showcase and guess what? When I arrived, all the posters had been changed and London Grammar were nowhere to be seen. Sub-Strokes Skaters, from New York, and nondescript waif-like songstress Nina Nesbitt were not adequate substitutes. If the Strypes don't turn up, I'm catching the next plane home, I thought. Oh me of little faith. Those nippers blew the place apart, their music like a mash-up of the Who and Dr Feelgood. My heart melted and I was transported back to my teens. Music ain't dead after all. They later proceeded to triumph at a series of bigger showcases and charm the likes of influential journalist David Fricke. Don't mess up, guys. (*They promptly did.)

As usual, I needed to find Hampshire bands. Southampton's Band Of Skulls had yet again moved on dramatically in status and were kicking off a high-profile US tour, with promotional posters attached to every Austin lamp post. So off I trekked (a really major one this, probably a couple of miles) to Bar 96, where I'd again got onto the guest list for yet another Filter showcase. And bloody hell, yet again the posters had been changed and they weren't there. It is infuriating when you make such detailed plans, merely to be thwarted for what I can only assume must be business reasons. Still, I did get to see Deap Vally, two Courtney Love-style scantily-clad rock chicks with spelling issues.

Thank goodness Public Service Broadcasting actually did appear in their scheduled slot at Latitude. They are a lorra fun - my only worry is that there's potential for them to be a one-trick pony. If you see them a few times, the amusement may wear off.

I really fancied the idea of seeing Gary Numan, so it was important to get to Brazos Hall (a new venue) early. Once again, this was a mistake, as the opening act (I don't know their name and I don't want to) was sub-operatic nonsense played at such ludicrous volume that people were literally running for the exits clutching their ears. I nearly had a fight with the sound engineer when I pointed out what was happening. He said I was too old to understand.

Luckily, Gary Numan was on top form, debuting strong new material (of course in the old style) and generally being a super-cool rock star. And after that, Blondie blasted out their greatest hits and some nice new songs too. Clem Burke (surrounded by plexiglass screens) is an absolutely incredible drummer. On the way home, we caught John Doe of X at the Continental, pretty much a Blondie contemporary, I'd guess. So that was what you might call a day of mixed fortunes.

In the morning, it was time to head to the Day Stage at Waterloo Records. I found myself absolutely loving Turin Brakes, of whom I knew nothing. They managed to produce the guitar solo of the week, and there's some pretty hot competition for that, I can tell you. Afterwards, Cate Le Bon charmed too, in quite a different way. But it was soon time to hit the annual Bloodshot Records party at the Yard Dog Gallery on South Congress. Ha Ha Tonka were just giving way to Lydia Loveless, who was excellent, like a punked-up Kathleen Edwards. It was a ridiculously crowded, wild and beer-soaked event, culminating in a soul/rock tour de force by Barrence Whitfield and the Savages, featuring a massive mosh pit and some failed crowd surfing (the bloke attempting it just fell flat on his back onto the concrete floor - ouch). Remember there was hardly a person there under fifty.

I planned to spend the entire evening at the Lou Reed tribute concert at the Paramount Theatre, but something wasn't quite right about it. It was extremely well-meant but somehow it didn't seem to be working. A really poor version of Perfect Day made the decision for us. So it was time for one more attempt at seeing London Grammar, this time at Stubb's. And it worked. They are rather sweet, very English and natural, in a slightly Portisheady kind of way. Their longevity will depend on how much more material they can come up with.

Saturday was going to be real Austin, a country rock day and nothing was going to stop me. No more chasing buzz acts. No entering of lotteries to see Coldplay, Jay-Z or Lady Gaga. It was off to the outskirts for the real thing. And what a treat was awaiting at the Broken Spoke. Tulsa singer-songwriter John Fullbright, performing to an attentive and packed front room, was my pick for the best solo performer of the week, with his beautiful songs and friendly wit. It's so rewarding when someone can spring a surprise like that.

At Alejandro Escovedo's annual Saturday party at Maria's, the beer is cold, the salsa is hot and the margaritas are lethal. But even by his own standards, he excelled himself with this bill. The Mastersons (effectively Steve Earle's backing band) have really tightened into a storming outfit with fine songs, while Garland Jefferies indulged his pleasure of marching into the crowd and barking into people's faces. It's more fun than it sounds. I absolutely adored the amazingly resilient BP Fallon, intoning poems rather than singing and backed by the amazing Austin electric duo The Ghost Wolves. Things like this you do not experience every day, and it feels such a privilege.

I love Jesse Malin. He seems to have been a bit quiet lately but I think that's about to change. Certainly, his electrifying set at Maria's, complete with a hot band and a bunch of very affecting new songs, indicated that a major comeback is on the cards. You could almost touch the excitement (so much so that I actually went back for more of him and BP Fallon the next evening at the Continental, after SXSW was theoretically over).

One notable thing about Jesse Malin's live shows was his willingness to give his all, physically charging around venues, diving into audiences and writhing on floors. I often thought this was potentially fraught with danger. I'm not sure if there is any connection - probably not - but in mid-2023 he suddenly suffered a rare spinal stroke that left him paralysed from the waist down. He subsequently underwent stem cell treatment in Argentina with the help of donations and benefit events from his thousands of fans and friends, and at the time of writing is reportedly on the way towards recovery.

And so to the journey home. A lovely, smooth and punctual flight. A seamless transfer to the National Express coach. On to the 69 bus to Twyford and … it broke down. Back to reality with a bump.

VENUE FOCUS: HOTEL SAN JOSE

The Hotel San Jose is situated on South Congress, diagonally opposite the Continental Club and adjacent to the iconic Austin Motel, whose phallic sign outside is an Austin landmark. Hotel San Jose has a large car park and this is where a mini-South By Southwest takes place each year. For the duration of the main festival, there is a programme of music all day, featuring surprisingly large acts, many of whom are also playing official showcases. It's quite an exposed area with no shade, so it's easy to get burnt in the heat. South By San Jose is a great gathering point but sometimes gets a trifle overcrowded. I have many memories of exciting performances at SXSJ, which include an unbelievably loud set from Mercury Rev, where the bass was so pronounced that the tarmac seemed to be vibrating. Another fun moment was when local icon Josh T Pearson was re-launching his career as a smooth, white-suited lounge lizard, unrecognisable from the previous version, which had featured a bushy beard down to his waist. After he had completed his own endearing set, he and his girlfriend proceeded to two-step through a rock and roll performance by another Texan hero, Jesse Dayton. An appreciative crowd gathered around Pearson and his partner, clapping on their every move and rather detracting from the activity on stage.

But it is for quite another reason that Hotel San Jose is forever imprinted on my memory. It all dates back to 2010, when I promoted a one-day Americana festival in Winchester, England. Wanting to pay tribute to South By Southwest, we had christened our promotions South By South Central, or SXSC for short, but this was the first time we had used the words 'South By' and 'Festival' in promotional material. This must have come to the attention of the South By Southwest organisers in Texas. Seemingly unmoved by the fact that ours was a tiny 100 capacity event on another continent, they clearly saw us as some kind of competition and sent me a very frightening letter, accusing us of breach of copyright and insisting that we cease and desist immediately. Thinking that this was either a joke or that they had completely misunderstood the nature of our event, I sent a pleasant and self-deprecating reply to them, suggesting that actually we were merely paying tribute to them and drawing people's attention to them. Back came a humourless and blunt rejection of my comments, expressed in dull but quite frightening legalese. The only thing I could now think of doing was to cave in and change our name, because according to the details of the document, South By Southwest owns the copyright to both the words South By and the letters SX, which didn't leave much scope. Anyway, back in Austin the following March, it suddenly struck me that South By San Jose was committing a similar sin to us and how, I wondered, could they get away with it? I walked up to the organisers' tent and inquired whether they had received similar threatening letters? "Oh those", laughed the lady in charge, "yeah, sure, we get one of those every year and just ignore them".

BANDS SEEN IN 2014

The Autumn Defense
Blondie
Hayes Carll
Deap Vally
John Doe
BP Fallon & The Ghost Wolves
The Felice Brothers
John Fullbright
Ha Ha Tonka
High As A Kite
Hurray For The Riff Raff
Garland Jeffreys
Cate Le Bon
London Grammar
Lydia Loveless
Jesse Malin

The Mastersons
James McMurty
Nina Nesbitt
Gary Numan
Public Service Broadcasting
Sturgill Simpson
The Skaters
Spandau Ballet
St. Vincent
Kelley Stoltz
The Strypes
Turin Brakes
Barrence Whitfield & The Savages

YEAR 13: 2015 / MARCH 17 - 21

Distilled from reviews in the Hampshire Chronicle,
Record Collector and Caught In The Act.

*In yet another attempt to find a new approach to reviewing SXSW,
this was an artist-by artist list of everyone we saw, in chronological
order.*
QUIET LIFE (Patagonia)

This was within 45 minutes of landing at Austin Bergstrom airport.
Quiet Life, from Portland, Oregon, entertained a range of families in
a clothes shop. Only in Austin ... *(Their guitarist Thor Jensen went
on to marry Glen Campbell's daughter Ashley).*

SONS OF BILL (Red 7)

A typical Red River dive. Over the road, a huge queue was trying
to get in to see local hero Gary Clark Jnr – and this was before the
festival had even officially started. SOB's good songs were slightly
blighted by a disinterested audience.

LAURA MARLING (Convention Center)

Major artists do little twenty-minute shows for the media during
the day in the Convention Center. It's always hard to generate any
atmosphere here but even taking that into account, this was a weak

performance, characterised by mistakes and fluffs and a piss-poor band. What do people see in her?

AMERICAN AQUARIUM (Dogwood)

A slightly sub-Springsteen performance by a hot new band from North Carolina. I spent most of the time trying to find some shade from the blazing sun.

FRANK TURNER (Cedar Street Courtyard)

See elsewhere.

MILKY CHANCE (Cedar Door)

Not the sort of band I normally would go and see - German hip-hop. But they were great and we benefited from loads of promotional freebies - I walked away with eleven pairs of sunglasses.

THE CRIBS (Clive Bar)

This involved a long walk, but I had a hankering for some nice melodic post-Ash power pop. Why bands like The Cribs bother to come to events like this I'm not sure, but I'm glad they do.

THE LOST BROTHERS (Capital Cruises)

No SXSW would be complete without a river cruise, and this one featured this friendly Irish duo and also Will Sexton (brother of Charlie). Great way to spend breakfast.

SUZY BOGGUSS (Broken Spoke)

Would never miss the annual Twangfest, held in Austin's most iconic venue. Straight country to two-step to.

AMY SPEACE (Broken Spoke)

She and her band had literally just arrived in Austin and were just getting going.

CHUCK PROPHET AND THE MISSION EXPRESS (Broken Spoke)

They just tore the place apart. This was the beginning of the slippery slope that led to us following Chuck around year after year, rather than actually reporting on other acts. They were so ridiculously good, it was impossible to resist.

JOSH SAVAGE (Steven F's bar)

A young singer from Winchester that I didn't mind bigging up, Josh acquitted himself admirably in the poshest of venues.

SKINNY LISTER (Lamberts)

I literally stuck a pin in the schedule and spotted a band name I recognised. Hugely impressed by their wildly uninhibited energy, including cider flagons and a crowd-surfing double bass player.

CHUCK PROPHET AND THE MISSION EXPRESS (Continental Club)

This was actually the least impressive Chuck show, because it was the official showcase and far too loud. However, the unexpected appearance of iconic rapper Bushwick Bill livened up proceedings.

BRONCHO (Hotel San Jose)

The heavy rain drove us to spend the whole afternoon here. It was a good decision. This was New Orderish post-punk from Oklahoma.

HOUNDMOUTH (Hotel San Jose)

I'd been hoping to see this stylish band and up they popped. They were on Letterman a week later.

THE ZOMBIES (Hotel San Jose)

Yes, you read that right. Sixties legends (especially in the States) sparked mass adulation in the drizzle. Who'd have thought that the best voice of SXSW 2015 would be Colin Blunstone? Totally fabulous singalong session.

SONS OF BILL (Lucky Lounge)

This is a super cool band but again, they suffered from a rowdy audience. One girl fell unconscious from her stool and crashed into me.

ANDREW COMBS (Lucky Lounge)

How sad that Ian McLagan (RIP) wasn't here to do his traditional Lucky Lounge shows. Andrew was fine but it's a strangely laid-out venue and I was glad to see him properly the next day.

CHUCK PROPHET AND THE MISSION EXPRESS
(Brooklyn Cantina)

Absolutely storming. Despite the cold and the rain and even a dud PA, they produced one of the most exciting shows I've ever seen. And you know, I've seen a lot. This one was enlivened by a stage-audience conversation about the rules of cricket during a break for equipment repairs.

DANIEL ROMANO (Brooklyn Cantina)

Laconic country stylings on the front porch of the same venue. They do cactus tacos and luscious beer here.

THE MASTERSONS (Brooklyn Cantina)

Officially the hardest-working duo of SXSW 2015, they are always cheerful and never flag.

DADDY LONGLEGS (Brooklyn Cantina)

If you have been missing the Legendary Shack*Shakers (I have), these are the guys for you.

ANDREW COMBS (Brooklyn Cantina)

This guy has a big future. I'm not going to say I'm wrong, because I still have high hopes.

CHUCK PROPHET AND THE MISSION EXPRESS (Continental Club)

I know it's ridiculous, but we simply hailed an Uber cab and followed them from venue to venue! I wonder what the US stalking laws are?

ELLIOTT BROOD (Swan Dive)

Always lovely to meet up with our Canuck pals. Shall we say, a certain amount of alcohol was consumed?

WHITEHORSE (Swan Dive)

Finished this year's SXSW with the ever-excellent Luke Doucet and Melissa McClelland in their new electronic format.

Of course, we also saw probably twenty more bands whose names we didn't catch (for example, several more on the boat trip). The next day was spent on a swing on Sarah Sharp's front porch in the sunshine. And then I flew home. I know I always say it, but this REALLY was the best one ever - mainly thanks to Chuck.

BANDS SEEN IN 2015

American Aquarium
Carl Barât
Courtney Barnett
Suzy Bogguss
Broncho
Andrew Combs
The Cribs
Daddy Longlegs
Elliott Brood
Gang of Four
Houndmouth
Elle King
Gill Landry
The Lost Brothers
Laura Marling
The Mastersons
Milky Chance
Motel Mirrors
Sam Outlaw
Chuck Prophet & The Mission Express
Quiet Life

Daniel Romano
Josh Savage
Doug Seegers
Will Sexton
Skinny Lister
Sons of Bill
Amy Speace
Turbo Fruit
Frank Turner
The Waco Brothers
Whiskey Shivers
Whitehorse
The Zombies

YEAR 14: 2016 / MARCH 15 - 19

Distilled from reviews in the Hampshire Chronicle,
Record Collector and Caught In The Act.

I started SXSW 2016 with a nasty throat infection, which I blamed on the vicious ventilation on the plane. Was that why I found the music less interesting this year? I don't think so, because it's a brilliant event and I had a huge amount of fun, but somehow things didn't click for me musically as much as usual.

First, all the good stuff. There were a couple of unique events that I'll never forget. One was a 'Song And Tell' session with Mercury Rev at the Ginger Man Pub. This took the form of Jonathan Donahue interviewing Bella Union's Simon Raymonde and the band performing - sublimely - three songs: Holes, All Is Dream and Opus 40. It's hard to describe how exciting it was to be close up with a band that more usually has to be approached through a mass of smoke and strobes. Indeed, that was the case just 24 hours later, as they performed a panoramic 90-minute greatest hits set at the Hotel San Jose. They must have frightened off the assembled Texans, because at the end, I turned round to see that two thirds of the audience had left. Lightweights.

The other extraordinary experience came courtesy of Timmy Thomas. At the age of seventy, and having spent the last 20 years teaching music, Timmy's career has experienced a sudden revival on account of Why Can't We Live Together being sampled by Drake.

Things got off to a strange start at Austin's iconic Saxon Pub with Timmy lecturing us about world peace for ten minutes, not realising his mic hadn't been switched on. But before long, his sublime band kicked in and hit a groove that had the place in ecstasy for an hour. It was such a privilege to be there.

Anyway, the whole point of SXSW is to check out new music and up-and-coming bands, so that is what I decided to do. It turned out to be less rewarding than I'd hoped, and I came home wondering whether music is in need of another punk-style shake-up.

First, some official showcases. The much touted Hinds were a bit of a laugh, a cross between the Bangles and the Slits but without the chops of either. Talk about ephemeral. On electronica, Poliça was a bit pompous and Chvrches had better jokes than music. It was time to go off-piste.

First I went to Maria's Taco Express. Like other such venues in Austin, SXSW uses it as an opportunity for band after band to play 30-minute sets with cursory sound checks. Performing here was Brian Whelan from LA, playing infectious bar room rock, greatly entertaining but not really going anywhere. Following on from him was veteran Canadian Corb Lund and his band. Again, the sardonic country songs were enjoyable but generic and you had the feeling of having heard it all before. Is it unreasonable to want to be thrilled and amazed?

The search continued by way of two sessions at the Ginger Man Pub in central Austin. This is a great venue but it's marred by a silly layout of extremely hard benches that run at right angles to the band, a sure recipe for a stiff neck. Here also, the format is an endless succession of bands that tune up, smash out six or seven three-minute guitar songs and disappear again. You only actually remember trivial things about them, such as that Blackfoot Gypsies had filthy trousers, Yoko And The Oh-Nos were a cross between ZZ Top and Boy George and that Soul Asylum should not try to perform their stadium anthems on acoustic guitars. You'd never consider buying a record by any of them. One band that stuck in the mind were called Dash Rip Rock. They came from Alabama and their songs included

Let's Go Fuck In My Truck and Spank Your Panties. It was alarming to be told that these weren't ironic titles. The Bluebonnets stood out on account of being women, but that was really the only difference.

Please don't get me wrong. None of these bands were bad as such. In fact, they could all play, they could all sing and rock out and they all had catchy songs and riffs. I went so far as to seek out the manager of the Ginger Man and congratulate him on the organisation. We didn't see a single bad band there, but of real spark, innovation and brilliance there was little sign. A vicious thunderstorm that closed down many outdoor venues didn't bother the Ginger Man, as, after a brief pause, they simply played on with yet another set of musos, this time some blisteringly loud, middle-aged rockers called The Sidewinders, who had forgotten they weren't punks any more. I couldn't bear to stay for the Waco Brothers, for fear it might be more of the same.

A lovely Saturday tradition is the Brooklyn Country Cantina, which showcases at least thirty roots / Americana bands over two stages. This is a great place to trawl for new talents, but not this year. David Wax Museum presented us with mock Mariachi, The Wild Reeds specialised in Coldplay-style soaring choruses, Christian Lee Hutson was trying to be Andrew Combs and failing, Banditos were more banjo-thrashing and throaty vocals and as for Sam Outlaw, oh dear. Bland, good-looking young country singers, I'm so fed up with them. Whatever else this may be (and it may be commercially successful), it isn't 'outlaw country'. That I could handle. Things were redeemed a little by Daddy Longlegs and Daniel Romano, but they had both played the year before and so weren't really 'new'.

Well, okay, as I said, I started SXSW with flu but I don't believe it tainted my experience and turned me into a grump. There definitely were positives to be found in the form of ubiquitous New Zealander Marlon Williams, whose songs actually sounded – phew, 'different', and Canada's Strumbellas. The band to watch out for out of all this is Saskatchewan's Kacy And Clayton, whose Fairport Convention fixation permits them to write beautiful tunes, and Kacy Lee Anderson had the voice of the week. In amongst all the rasping growls and yells of the other bands, her sweet, innocent, Sandy Denny-ish tones stood out a mile.

BANDS SEEN 2016

Banditos
Blackfoot Gypsies
Blue Healer
The Bluebonnets
Chvrches
Dash Rip Rock
David Wax Museum
Nina Diaz
Javier Escovedo
BP Fallon with Joe King Carrasco
Robbie Fulks
Golden Dawn Arkestra
Hinds
Horse Thief
Christian Lee Hutson
Jenifer Jackson
The Jason James Band
Kacy & Clayton
Corb Lund
Loretta Lynn
Mercury Rev
Money Mothers
Mothers
Michael Martin Murphy
Sam Outlaw
Rozi Plain
Polica
Iggy Pop
Daniel Romano

Sarah Sharp
The Sidewinders
Soul Asylum
The Strumbellas
Timmy Thomas
Brian Whelan
The Wild Reeds
Marlon Williams
Yoko & The Oh-Nos

YEAR 15: 2017 / MARCH 14 - 18

Distilled from reviews in Record Collector,
Caught In The Act and Americana UK.

Yet another new writing outlet presented itself this year. A super website called Americana-UK.com had been around for a while and with the rise of Americana appreciation in the UK had started getting substantial visitor numbers. It's a great site and does a superb job because it has a nicely catholic approach to the concept of Americana, being tolerant and inclusive of a range of music types as well as also left of centre politically and not afraid to say so. I suggested the idea of doing a SXSW diary for them and it has now turned into an annual tradition. Because a website is not restricted spacewise like a magazine is, creating the need for highly condensed coverage, AUK presents me with the ideal platform for my uncontrolled verbosity.

SXSW has got its mojo back after overcrowding and over-corporatism had changed the vibe in recent years. I also got my own mojo back this year with the help of a better selection of artists, familiarity with great and cheap eating places and a week of uninterrupted sunshine.

I'll be clear: I had decided this would be my last SXSW. After fifteen consecutive years and with a bad ankle that made the traditional lengthy hikes a real challenge, this was to be the end. Now I'm not quite sure.

A new policy sought to avoid the endless walking. It entailed selecting events in advance to go to and simply stay put. This was possible thanks to Paul, who has conveniently become a non-drinker and therefore was willing and able to drive us around. The only issue was parking, but even in this we managed to get lucky most of the time.

The sun blazed on our necks at Waterloo Records as Hurray For The Riff Raff played one of their eight shows, Beach Slang came up with some very entertaining lighthearted grunge, Robyn Hitchcock and Emma Swift demonstrated their mutual devotion and Modern English, on a 'comeback' tour, were hysterically pompous and dreadful. A quick visit to the atmospheric Ginger Man pub downtown for a nice encounter with Tom Heyman was followed by a very rewarding evening at Easy Tiger.

This event was the twentieth anniversary of Bella Union, in my opinion the best record label in the world. How exciting it was to experience BNQT, which was Midlake joined by Jason Lytle and Travis's Fran Healey for a joyful run through of their various hits, plus some new songs too. Other artists playing included Oklahoma's excellent Horse Thief, and it was intriguing to observe label boss Simon Raymonde and his wife Abbi bopping along to every single act with endless enthusiasm. Their dedication to music is all too clear.

The next day saw a visit to Yard Dog Gallery on South Congress. A common characteristic of all the places I am describing is the superhuman amount of alcohol consumed. I'm by no means teetotal but I tell you, the amount these guys put away is mind-boggling. Nursing a three-dollar local IPA, I was hugely entertained by a highly-wired Austin Lucas (whose Alone In Memphis always brings a lump to the throat). After that, the place was trashed by an incredible band from Philadelphia called Low Cut Connie, whose singer Adam Weiner spent most of his time leaping on and off his piano and into the audience, while his band crouched and prowled around him. Not since the Jim Jones Revue at the Mean Eyed Cat has such a seedy and dangerous boogie groove been heard in Austin.

Could that be topped? Oh yes, with the supercharged political punk of Lee Bains III and the Glory Fires, music at its most primal and at the same time its most intelligent.

That evening saw one of the few Americana showcases taking place in a central venue. It was that of New West records, a label with an enviable roster of talent. Laying out their wares were the Secret Sisters (how must they feel now that sweet-voiced duos have become such an overcrowded market?) and Sara Watkins (slightly troubled by intermittent power cuts). Andrew Combs caused confusion - at least to me - by performing with Cale Tyson's backing band (see below). Some members of the Deslondes used to be in Hurray For The Riff Raff and continue to pursue that rootsy direction with skill and energy. HFRR, meanwhile, have long since moved on from Americana showcases and were displaying their new political indie-rock direction at bigger events all over the city. The much-anticipated Aaron Lee Tasjan started on a tremendous high but rapidly declined into a set of bafflingly bland material that belied his flamboyant image.

The Americana highlight of my SXSW was, as always, Saturday's annual Brooklyn Country Cantina at Licha's Cantina, curated by 'Bug' Jenkins of the Defibulators. Cale Tyson and his (other) band brought things to a rousing climax (apparently he has different bands for different regions) but for me the highlight of the day, and indeed the whole festival, was a highly-emotional and deeply affecting twenty-minute set from Nashville's Langhorne Slim. They don't come better.

During that evening, I was gripped by a desire to nip to the nearby Hotel Vegas to see The Sloths, an ancient band of shock-rockers who'd reunited for SXSW. This was because we'd recently become sloth enthusiasts on a family visit to Costa Rica. The Sloths were hilarious (and I also bumped into the multi-talented Rusty Miller, from California). At one stage, I found a place to perch and try to make sense of the surrounding madness. Four deafeningly loud bands were blasting out from four stages all around, the sound melding into the craziest cacophony imaginable. Everyone in the crowd was drunk, drugged up and chaotically, blissfully happy. To most people, it would have been hell on earth. To me, with my unstoppable music addiction, it was classic SXSW and the purest bliss.

Here's something that also happened that year but I didn't write about at the time because it seemed too raw. It says a lot about my relationship with SXSW and Austin in general.

Never in a million years would I have dreamt of even meeting Ian McLagan, far less having any kind of relationship with him. To me he was a superstar, having played with the magnificent Small Faces for so many years, before working with the Faces, Rolling Stones, Bob Dylan and numerous other huge acts. I pictured him living in a Beverley Hills mansion with an extravagant lifestyle, but that was before I read his autobiography All The Rage, which sets out in all too graphic detail the way in which he had been ripped off by the industry all the way through his long and distinguished career. I knew that he had eventually settled in Austin with his wife (and Keith Moon's ex) Kim and was happily making music with local chums in the famously music-orientated city. He truly seemed to have found his place of destiny.

One day, to my amazement, I got offered a show in Winchester by Ian and his Bump Band on a European tour. With no hope of a positive outcome and aware that I was taking on a financial commitment way above anything I'd ever dared before, I put in a pitch. I think our chances had been improved by the fact that we had previously played host to the Resentments, an Austin supergroup who shared a couple of band members with Ian's Bump Band. The Resentments still, to this day, play every Sunday evening at the Saxon pub in Austin. Ian's arrival at the Railway in Winchester was marked by the extraordinary experience of having to take the stage door off its hinges in order to squeeze his signature Hammond B3 through it. The show was just magnificent, but I'm pretty certain it must have been a loss-making tour because the next time we were offered a show by Ian it was as a duo with an Austin bass guitarist called Jon Notarthomas.

When they arrived, it was clear that one of John's principal rôles was to be Mac's minder, a kind of benevolent father figure, despite his being at least twenty years his junior. There was a palpable connection between the two. I am pleased to say that I became friends with Jon on that day and remain so now. However, there was also another obscure connection that I had not suspected. When Laura Veirs played for us and I told her keyboard player Steve Morse that I planned to go to Austin in 2003, he made me promise to go to a hot dog stand called Best Wurst that would be visible on 6th Street. He assured me it would be the best hot dog I had ever eaten, so I didn't have the heart to tell him that I was vegetarian.

It wasn't until meeting Jon Notarthomas in Winchester that I realized that he was in fact the owner of the Best Wurst franchise, which had a collection of hot dog stands positioned in various places around the city and did indeed have the reputation of extremely high quality. We now need to fast forward to the year 2006, when Mac's wife Kim had been tragically killed in a car crash in Travis County. It seemed evident that Mac was coping with that by throwing himself into huge amounts of work in Texas. I had been lucky enough to see him and Jon in various incarnations at successive SXSWs and joined the rest of the music world in mourning, as Ian himself unexpectedly died of a stroke in 2014. Jon, as his honorary kind uncle in the absence of any family available locally, had to take on responsibility for trying to sort out Ian's affairs after his death.

To my astonishment, Jon invited me to spend the day with him as I waited for my plane on the Sunday after the end of South By Southwest 2017. He drove me out to Ian's ranch about 30 miles outside Austin, and then on to the lockup where all his gear was being stored. I don't think Jon could ever have appreciated just how totally gobsmacked I was to find myself in this position, because Ian had been one of my ultimate rock and roll heroes, whom I held in enormous awe. Among the amps, keyboards and sundry bits and pieces in the lockup were several of Ian's artworks, created in the midst of the debilitating migraines from which he suffered in the latter years of his life. Jon, who was in the process of deliberating what to do with all these artefacts, simply invited me to choose one of those paintings to take with me. I'm proud to say that it now hangs on the wall of my office at home.

Meanwhile, this was the actual day when final negotiations were taking place for Jon to sell the Best Wurst franchise to another company and I admit that I was a slightly nervous passenger, as he spent most of the journey in his pickup talking animatedly into his mobile phone rather than concentrating on the road. I was actually with him when the deal went through, causing much joy (which I believe was relatively short-lived because the people that bought the business didn't make much of a success of it). I will always be grateful for Jon for the privilege that he gave me and each year when we go to Austin, we make sure to check out one of the many bands that Jon plays in.

VENUE FOCUS: CEDAR STREET COURTYARD

Occasionally I am pressed into committing myself to an answer to the question, "What is your favourite venue in Austin?" Certainly, from the point of view of exciting musical experiences in the past, it has to be the Cedar Street Courtyard. Centrally situated, it is an ideal place for live music, with a high stage and good sight lines. It also has a compact and cosy feel and benefits from a staircase leading down to the stage, which is ideal for spectacular entrances and exits (Ricky Wilson slid down the banister). Paul and I discovered early on that Cedar Street has a similar characteristic to Stubb's, in that if you sneak around through the bar on the right hand side, you can emerge through a door that brings you out actually at the lip of the stage. Although this has the disadvantage that you find yourself directly in front of the extraordinarily loud speakers, it does mean that you are extremely close to the performers, many of whom are big stars who you'd never get to bathe in the sweat of otherwise. Documented elsewhere in this book is the chaotic admissions procedure, which we could certainly do without, and the fact that in 2023 it was colonised by the British contingent, meaning that the big star names are no longer featured. But we were the lucky ones, being able to experience acts like Primal Scream (2008 – I was able to look up Bobby Gillespie's nose, which was educational), Billy Bragg, Keane, Kaiser Chiefs and, on one particularly glorious occasion, the Bangles. Being within inches of Susanna Hoffs was one of the highlights of my life.

BANDS SEEN IN 2017

Michaela Anne
Lee Bains III & The Glory Fires
Beach Slang
BNQT
Andrew Combs
The Deslondes
Grandaddy
Tom Heyman
Robyn Hitchcock & Emma Swift
Horse Thief
Hurray For The Riff Raff
Langhorne Slim
Low Cut Connie
Austin Lucas
The Mastersons
Modern English
Secret Sisters
The Sloths
Spoon
Aaron Lee Tasjan
Cale Tyson
Sara Watkins

YEAR 16: 2018 / MARCH 13 - 17

Distilled from reviews in Record Collector,
Caught In The Act and Americana UK.

Here's the full blow-by-blow. I only do it because my memory is going and I want something to refer to to help me look back in years to come.

The music festival has been starting earlier each year and now they even list Tuesday in the official booklet, despite the dates actually being Wednesday to Saturday. I picked up my badge from the Convention Center, where it was noticeable that the traditional queues were completely absent. The general 'quieter than usual' feel continued throughout the festival. What has happened is that the big names have almost completely disappeared (the biggest stars were Keith Urban and a secret show by ZZ Top). The result is a return to the original ethos of SXSW as a showcase for new talent.

We tried to find a parking space to start checking out the music early but failed, opting instead to pay a first visit to Guero's before having an early night. Planning SXSW in detail is essential and I'd done my homework in advance, ready to leap straight in. All bands play multiple shows. You see them pitch up in their vans, lug all their own gear on stage, set everything up, do a cursory sound check if they're lucky, play an energetic set and instantly vacate the stage with all their gear as the next band is already setting up. It's an object lesson in professionalism. There are no dressing rooms or riders for these people.

We aimed to start at around 1pm each day, which left time for breakfast in Star Seeds Café. This was normally the only meal of the day, further nutrition being taken in the form of beers and margaritas.

Wednesday was largely spent at South By San Jose. An early highlight was Josh T Pearson, about whom I'd read a huge article in Uncut on the way over. Josh was on rollicking form with his new crowd-pleasing image. Despite his popularity in Europe, he's almost unknown in his home town, with the audience at Hotel San Jose being sparse. It was great fun and he finished off with a cover of a Neil Halstead song, before complimenting me on my John Murry t-shirt. If you look into their respective life stories, it's no surprise that these two should like each other.

Straight after Josh came Jesse Dayton. Despite having the aura of a Texas road warrior, Jesse is in fact a sensitive, deep-thinking individual as well as a spectacular guitar player with an unimpeachable band. Next door, Guero's garden was overflowing with adoring fans awaiting the arrival of Frank Turner. Everyone in the rammed venue knew all the lyrics and sang along enthusiastically, even when he was exhorting them to "Make America Great Again". He had another eight shows to go, so disappeared quickly afterwards.

Antone's is a much more intimate venue since its move across town, but an improved one too, with good sound and sightlines. I was excited because Joshua Hedley, a man who has played in my garden, has been signed to Jack White's Third Man label and was showcasing here. It was a trifle embarrassing because it was so 'straight country' that Paul hated it. Myself, I was in awe of the incredible collection of Nashville musos (in uniforms) that Joshua had brought with him, and loved the smooth professionalism of it all.

In order to carry out my duty of checking out Hampshire artists, I went to the relaxing confines of the Central Presbyterian Church for Portsmouth singer Jerry Williams, who'd crowdfunded her trip. It's probably rude to say that I can't remember any of her songs, but it's also true. Next up was Winchester's Flyte, the brother of one of whose members went to school with my daughter (hope you're following this). They feature CSNY-style harmonies and are normally an electric band, but on this occasion they went acoustic with a grand piano and it all sounded suitably ecclesiastical.

Having loved Low Cut Connie at last year's festival, it was vital to go and see them at least once. This was a show in the bedlam of 6th Street at a long-established venue called The Parish. The sound was too loud, the lights too flashy and somehow the vibe wasn't quite right, but nevertheless we were knocked out by Oklahoma's Broncho, who had become even more crazy since we had spotted them the year before. More of both these two later. Bed was at 2.30 am.

Thursday started with a visit to the calm and comfortable Day Stage in the Convention Center. Considering that Courtney Marie Andrews is a very fast-rising star, the number of people there was tiny. The environment suited her, though, and she performed a short but effective set. Some reviews have pointed out that there's little variation in her strong-lunged approach to each song, and it's true but it's fine by me.

At the Day Stage at the legendary Waterloo Records, A Place To Bury Strangers made the most wonderful racket. Then came the most unlikely ever signing to the country-focused New West label, a feisty pop band led by Caroline Rose. Dressed in sports gear and medical scrubs, they entertained the crowd cheerfully. The Weather Station, who played numerous shows over the weekend, were less memorable, but not as dire as the turgidly dated sub-Coldplay anthems of Dashboard Confessional. Ugh. Time for some much-needed healthy food at the adjacent branch of Whole Foods.

A long walk back downtown took me to an Irish showcase in the tiny Velveeta Room on Sixth Street. Here is a good point to mention something that has been increasingly clear in recent years, namely a sort of involuntary segregation that has been developing. Sixth Street has become the hub for urban and rap music, while the traditional venues featuring more rock-style music have largely dispersed themselves along Rainey Street and East Fourth Street, both endowed with scores of bars with music facilities.

The Irish showcase was extremely enjoyable and a good advert for tolerance, taste and good behaviour in a music venue. First up was a spiky punk trio from Derry with Undertones undertones, called Touts. I could have been their grandfather, and would have been proud to be. One of their songs was called Go Fuck Yourself. Next up was the acoustic harmony duo The Lost Brothers. I was fearful they'd die a death but no, the audience listened respectfully and appreciatively to their music. Finally, The Strypes generally laid waste to the place with their attitude-laden Feelgood-ish chunky, melodic two-minuters. They've invested in some great threads and look perfect. I was convinced when I first saw them here four years ago that they'd be huge, but they aren't. Maybe it's just true that there is no market for guitar bands any more.

A long and bracing walk took us to Rainey Street and a Tulsa showcase at The Bungalow. I feared the worst as a pop act called Branjae was playing and was worried for John Fullbright, who was following and I'd only ever seen solo before. No need to worry though, as he was playing with a bunch of friends and it was a very cheerful gathering. It was noticeable, however, that the momentum dipped whenever a friend came up to play and re-gathered pace whenever Fullbright took the lead, with his vocal and instrumental power. And what's this? Yes, it's Broncho again. You could hardly imagine a greater musical contrast. In my search for a way to describe them, I came up with 'a mash-up of My Bloody Valentine, The Jesus And Mary Chain and Hawkwind'. Add in a bit of The Cure (singer Ryan Lindsey is a dead ringer for Robert Smith) and you have a potent and very atmospheric cocktail, as Lindsey jiggles as if flea-ridden, sings lyrics which may or may not be actual words and merges each song into the next with no breaks for applause or even a greeting. Anyway, Paul and I found them so irresistible that we went to see them three times in total.

Friday saw me wending my way again to Rainey Street for a showcase at Blackheart that I hoped would be headlined by Ezra Furman. What a pig's ear the organisers had made of this. There was a spacious yard outside with a stage, yet they had programmed Ezra Furman and Frank Turner in the minuscule and very claustrophobic inside room. Luckily, that meant I was unhindered while watching Aaron Lee Tasjan outside. The previous year, I had been baffled by a low-key and - dare I say it - boring show from Aaron, and confused by the adulation. Here at Blackheart, he was in his electric guitar-shredding guise and the performance was thrilling. Clearly a man of many and diverse talents.

Amy Shark and a couple of other forgettable artists played outside but I ventured in to try and get a spot to at least catch a glimpse of Ezra Furman, but it was not to be. His band and crew dutifully set up all the gear but the frantic onstage phone calls gave a clue as to what would happen: He simply didn't turn up. An announcement gave mixed messages: He's not well, but do come and see him (in a bigger venue) tomorrow. Who knows the explanation but I'd guess the overcrowding must have been an intimidatory factor. Never mind, normally SXSW throws up many of these situations (indeed, for many, it later did, with cancellations relating to security issues).

We had a date with Lee Bains III And The Glory Fires (who played, I think, eleven times over the four days). This was at the Side Bar, next to Stubb's, and turned out to be a classic SXSW occasion. Inside the dingy venue was a set-up for bands that offered neither stage nor lights, so it was only possible to see the silhouettes of Cold Fronts, a great Pavement-esque outfit from Philadelphia. Outside on the sun-drenched patio, Lee Bains was on paint-stripping form. For me, he took the title of Best Band I Saw At SXSW This Year (a rather subjective category, admittedly). Hurling himself round the tiny stage and challenging the audience with incredibly articulate political speeches and lyrics, Lee eventually ended up in the audience being mobbed by the ecstatic crowd. Wonderful in-yer-face stuff that made you feel glad to be alive and able to feel positive in a difficult world.

What a contrast the evening was. A friend of my daughter's was organising a showcase in St David's Historic Sanctuary, so of course I attended. The artist I saw was Lucy Rose. Fair play to her. She's been through the industry mill, having been hyped by a major label to little avail. The current angle is that she's now independent and succeeding against the odds, but boy, was her performance bland and inconclusive. But pay no attention to me, the audience lapped it up.

Next was a hike all the way to the wonderful Scoot Inn, where the musical quality was outstanding. I'd fallen in love with Austin's Bright Light Social Hour on the Tropical Heatwave Cruise and it was lovely to see them wowing their home town. I feared for Hiss Golden Messenger when I saw that it was an acoustic duo set-up, but no, yet again they were treated with respect and attention by a well-oiled party audience. You don't get that everywhere. Last on were Okkervill River. Yes, they exist again, nowadays in a completely different and much more quirky (but appealing) five-piece format.

The plan for Saturday was to take things a bit more easy. First up was Lucy's Fried Chicken, a venue that always has an entertaining line-up. The problem is that it is what it says: If you don't like fried chicken you're going to starve. They don't even do tea or coffee. Also, the sightlines are bad, so it's not the best place to see a band. But I wanted to be there because of the Rubilators, the new band of Jon Notarthomas. I was glad we made the effort, as the Rubilators are a bunch of enthusiastic Austin veterans who rock out with infectious style. After them came John Doe (of X), who has now made Austin his home and has a new acoustic trio.

Chickengate meant that we did the ultimate in sinfulness, namely having beer and margaritas for breakfast, back in Guero's. Just up the road is the Yard Dog. Normally we'd spend a lot of time in there but the crowds made it impossible even to see local act Li'l Cap'n Travis, although they sounded good from a distance. So instead it was off to the other side of town to the traditional Saturday Country Cantina at Licha's. The line-up was less inspiring than in recent years but we saw Billy Strings, Dead Horses and Australia's Ruby Boots in quick succession.

Back in town we entered a rather smart bar to see Welsh songwriter Christopher Rees, who'd been having a trying time on account of a banister-related ankle incident. Nevertheless, he was in fine voice. He's one of the very few UK Americana artists who sounds really authentic.

The last evening was shaping up to develop into a disappointment. For years we'd been going to showcases organised by Canadian label Six Shooter, but the bigger they've become, the less fun the events are. This one contained many irritating factors: A cliquey atmosphere, people annoyingly smoking everywhere, sound leakage from next door, massively over-priced drinks, terrible sound plus a self-consciously quirky and not very good band (The Wet Secrets). Tempting though it was to stay on for Whitney Rose (simply so I could call this article The Wars Of The Roses on account of the many so-named singers), the temptation of another dose of Broncho and Low Cut Connie in the adjacent Clive Bar was too great.

And what a wise decision that proved to be. The vibe, with free St Patrick's Day light sabres and flashing necklaces, was incredibly convivial and Broncho were even more mind-boggling than before. Low Cut Connie, meanwhile, were back at their sparkling best. The extraordinary Adam Weiner of LCC took the showmanship honours for the week with his piano acrobatics and gradual disrobement, backed by a grittily committed bunch of highly supportive musicians. They all certainly know how to work an audience and the audience succumbs willingly, wreathed in smiles. I saw Rolling Stone's David Fricke (who really has seen everything) being clearly overcome. In print, he declared the band and their new single Beverley to be ready for world domination. I can only agree.

That was it. Bed and the long trek to a snowy home via Amsterdam presented a climate challenge, but that's another story.

BANDS SEEN IN 2018

A Place To Bury Strangers
Courtney Marie Andrews
Lee Bains III & The Glory Fires
The Paul Benjamin Band
Ruby Boots
Branjae

The Bright Light Social Hour
Broncho
Cold Fronts
Dashboard Confessional
Jesse Dayton
Dead Horses
John Doe
Flyte
John Fullbright
Joshua Hedley
Hiss Golden Messenger
The Lost Brothers
Low Cut Connie
Okkervil River
Josh T. Pearson
Chuck Prophet & The Mission Express
Red Dirt Rangers
Christopher Rees
Caroline Rose
Lucy Rose
The Rubilators
Amy Shark
Billy Strings
The Strypes
Aaron Lee Tasjan
Touts
L'il Cap'n Travis
Frank Turner
The Weather Station
The Wet Secrets
Jerry Williams

YEAR 17: 2019 / MARCH 12 - 16

Distilled from reviews in Record Collector,
Caught In The Act and Americana UK.

One piece of received wisdom regarding SXSW is that it has become over-corporate and is no longer worth attending for an Americana fan. This I would refute strongly. It's true that it was heading that way a few years ago, but the organisers have pulled back and taken the festival back to its roots as a showcase for new and established bands. The 'big names' and overcrowding have stopped and the experience is just brilliant. If you are tempted to head to SXSW, then you should. Maybe a few details about how it all works will help you decide.

A hindrance in the past was getting from venue to venue, but the arrival of Uber and the ubiquitous electric scooters have changed all that. Those pesky scooters will eventually need some kind of regulation (there are thousands of them everywhere) but they are dead useful (if slightly anarchic).

Examples of great city centre venues include Cooper's Barbecue, which featured a series of record company showcases, with performances by Erin Rae and Cedric Burnside, as well as the Single Lock label's owner John Paul White of the Civil Wars. He started well with a hint of Roy Orbison but disappointingly descended into generic country rock. Cooper's played host to my favourite show this year (as last year), a politically-charged and highly emotional rock tour de force from Alabama's Lee Bains III And The Glory Fires.

South by San Jose was this year celebrating its 20th year with strong performances from the likes of Robert Ellis, resplendent in white tuxedo in his new Texas Piano Man guise. Hayes Carll presented his new album here but there were disappointing performances from Edie Brickell And The New Bohemians (standard AOR) and E.B. The Younger (bland and dull, quite astonishing considering he also leads Midlake).

The other unmissable event is the Luck Reunion, a stellar one-day festival held on Willie Nelson's ranch, thirty miles outside Austin. The sun blazed down on a total of seven stages of varying sizes, one of them in a saloon and another in a chapel. The country stars were out in force, including Steve Earle, doing his Guy Clark covers, Mavis Staples and sundry members of the Nelson family. The Revival Tent was particularly exciting, with spectacular shows from Low Cut Connie and the inimitable Nude Party, who also curated a great little stage in the beer garden full of chunky garage bands. The Mavis Staples Stage hosted the huge-lunged Courtney Marie Andrews and Bristol newcomer Yola. In the US, either they'll take to her soul infections or they won't. It will be interesting to see.

Pretty much everywhere you go will be noisy and lively, but there are also a few 'listening rooms' where rapt audiences will pay close attention to quiet performers. One such venue is the back room at the Townsend on Congress, where Austinite Will Johnson (of Centro-Matic / South San Gabriel) gave an intense performance with his trio. At Maria's Taco Express, still hanging in there, we caught London's hard-working Curse Of Lono and an outstanding, pleasantly noisy band from South Carolina called the Artisanals.

You can also, if the mood takes you, chase the new 'buzz' bands. This year the most exciting one was Dublin's astonishing Fontaines DC. To be sure of getting in, we arrived at BD Riley's two hours early, which was a good move because it allowed us to catch some great Irish acts such as Whenyoung. As for Fontaines DC, they are an amalgamation of the Fall and the Blue Aeroplanes, with a chunk of Whipping Boy and a hint of Lee Brilleaux. Sounds good? You bet it was.

One particularly amazing experience was enjoying a spectacular set of bonkers psychedelia from the Crazy World Of Arthur Brown. Arthur lived in Austin for 16 years and his band consists of crack Texas musos, led by the Resentments' Bruce Hughes.

This was a day on which yet another new and unexpected aspect of my sxsw coverage was put to the test. A new editor had arrived at Record Collector magazine and came up with the bright idea of starting each month's Live reviews with a main feature. This was to contain a live photograph, a review of the concert, a brief interview with the performer and - this was the difficult bit - a photograph of the artist together with the writer - in this case, me.

I have no idea what the thinking behind this was but I generally feel that publishing a photograph of a writer alongside an article is a redundant thing to do. Nonetheless, my aforementioned vanity and ambition with regard to music journalism made the temptation of bagging the main slot on the Live page irresistible, so I set out with alacrity to make the necessary arrangements. Prior to applying it in Austin, I had already had dry runs with Mark King of Level 42, who was plainly not remotely interested but felt obliged, and Mark Everett of Eels, who was as grumpy as you might expect. More successful altogether was a very friendly encounter with Kim Simmonds of Savoy Brown, who sounded me out about maybe ghosting his autobiography, only to sadly drop dead within the year. These less than inspiring results were not surprising, because being accosted and interviewed either immediately before or after an energetic live performance is surely not an appealing prospect for any artist, and posing for a selfie probably the final straw. Anyway, on this day in Austin, I had my eyes set on the legendary Arthur Brown to be my victim for this year's sxsw coverage. A very friendly and cooperative management team helped me set up the arrangements, which inevitably entailed me waiting for nearly two hours while they sound checked, but things worked out brilliantly. The show was being steered by Arthur's son, who lives in Austin. and it turned out that I knew one of the musicians in Arthur's band.

The performance was incendiary, absolutely brilliant for someone of any age, far less Arthur's advanced years, and he himself was an absolute delight, posing cheerfully in his make-up and regalia and nattering away about his memories of the Isle of Wight.

Getting to the encounter was quite difficult because we had to drive in from many miles away in Texas Hill country, where we had been attending Willie Nelson's Luck Reunion on his ranch. This also threw up one or two anomalies for our coverage, in that we had been actively encouraged and courted to attend by the promotions company responsible for plugging it. Indeed, it was a thrilling experience that we would have loved to repeat. I kind of took it for granted that it would be possible to attend again in future years but it turned out to be a completely closed shop, and negotiating the elaborate levels of bureaucracy required to gain admission proved so daunting that we have never managed to engineer a return.

BANDS SEEN IN 2019

Courtney Marie Andrews
The Artisanals
Lee Bains III & The Glory Fires
Edie Brickell & The New Bohemians
Broncho
The Crazy World Of Arthur Brown
Cedric Burnside
Hayes Carll
Curse Of Lono
E.B. The Younger
Robert Ellis
Fontaines D.C.
Will Johnson
Low Cut Connie
Nude Party

Erin Rae
Whenyoung
John Paul White
Yola

2020: COVID – NO LIVE SXSW

YEAR 18: 2021 / MARCH 16 - 20
THE 'VIRTUAL' YEAR

The organisers decided to take the whole event online in order to combat the Covid travel ban, and I joined in enthusiastically.

Distilled from reviews in Record Collector,
Caught In The Act and Americana UK.

Negotiating the South By South West Festival normally entails walking for miles, staying up very late and dealing with blisters, drunkenness and severe confusion as to who is playing where and when. It's the most wonderful experience but it obviously couldn't take place in its usual form this year. SXSW online presented its own quandaries and mysteries.

The first one was working out exactly who was playing and at what time, a severe challenge for a non-mathematically-minded viewer in the UK. The techies at SXSW had created five channels you could choose from, but I discovered very quickly that the schedule wasn't that well suited to someone watching from Europe. Generally, shows started around 10 pm, running through to about 4 am. "Hmm, okay," I thought, "I'll take up the challenge," and set myself up in front of my computer for an all-night marathon. This went badly wrong on the very first evening, when I misinterpreted the schedule. Normally at the real SXSW, shows start at 7 pm and go through till about 2 am and are listed as being on the day the shows start, i.e. if the show is at 1 am on Thursday morning it is included in Wednesday's listings. I do hope you're following this. My assumption that this would be the case proved to be inaccurate, as tuning in in anticipation of Canada's Holy Fuck and NYC's A Place To Bury Strangers revealed itself to be 24 hours after the shows had actually taken place, and I was left staring at a static and inactive screen. Luckily, a few enquiries revealed that it was possible to do a catch-up the next day although again, it was extremely difficult to work out exactly what time the showcases would be happening.

Another anomaly was the fact that most of the showcases were presented by various management companies and each show was listed both individually and as part of the showcase. It normally wasn't possible to work out what order the bands would be appearing in and at exactly what time. This was particularly apparent in the showcase featuring Reverend Peyton's Big Damn Band, The Wandering Hearts and a few others. Who would be up next was anybody's guess.

Years ago, I got myself into trouble for being rude about The Wandering Hearts so I thought I'd give them another go. My revised opinion, having viewed their front room show, is that they are another of those 'pleasant' harmony acoustic trios and quite harmless. But when you put them next to a barnstorming, blockbusting band such as Reverend Peyton, ... well, it does, I suppose, all go to prove how all-inclusive the Americana tag can be.

Giving up on the plan of making a schedule which became even more complicated then actually physically traipsing from venue to venue, I was able to take the opportunity to check out some things I never would have normally, such as some fabulous bands from Spain (Belako and the XTC-ish Alien Tango), a cool bunch from Australia and, of course, Ireland (the fabulously ethereal Aiofe Nessa Frances and the intriguing Pillow Queens). The ability to flip from screen to screen and not have to stand in a queue and produce ID was a definite advantage in these circumstances. It was, however, quite peculiar not to have the normal gig anticipation excitement of watching the crew setting up the gear, testing the mics etc. All you got was a blank screen with some kind of logo as you waited in trepidation to see whether the band you wanted to see is actually going to appear or whether you have misinterpreted the advance information.

Then, when the band actually is performing, you realise suddenly just what it is that makes the online experience so different from the in-person one, namely the proliferation of camera angles and close-ups. Your normal view is from in front of the stage, where you can see the entire band. In order to replicate the on-screen experience in a live venue, you'd have to climb up onto the ceiling or jump on stage and position yourself inches away from the artist. I definitely prefer the real live thing, but nonetheless would like to give massive credit to the creators of the online festival for the huge effort they put in to try to make it realistic. On some occasions, such as the British Music Embassy, they did get very near indeed to the real experience by filming at tremendous volume in a dingy club environment. This meant that punk acts such as Chubby And The Gang could come into their own and Penelope Isles could make a really deep impression.

Thursday evening offered the opportunity to toggle between Irish artists (traditionally the Texans' favourites) and some great Texan artists (normally loved by the Irish) including American Dreamer and Betty Soo. She initially won the 'most spectacular mask' prize for five minutes until being upstaged by Como Las Movies, whose face-covering took the form of an octopus, since you ask. With music as good as this, it could get frustrating that most sets were only two or three songs long.

The conference aspect of SXSW proceeded as usual, largely in a Zoom format. I dipped into conversations with Brian Eno, plus the 88-year-old Willie Nelson (he gets everywhere but not even he could stage his annual Luck Reunion this year) and an engrossing chat with the impossibly cool Ron and Russell Mael of Sparks. Sadly, a prevalent theme of many discussions was how to rescue live music.

Americana fans were treated to a fine Saturday. Spiky Texan Carson McHone and her super-cool band including Hammond and neatly distorted guitars delivered one of my personal high points of the week - lovers of Kathleen Edwards should keep a close eye on Carson. A poignant set by The Deer from the stage of the Continental Club, featuring the guitar solo of the week from guitarist Michael McLeod, led up to veteran Austin icon Jon Dee Graham at the same venue with his son William. Nothing could stop these two, displaying inter-generational guitar duelling at its finest. Black Joe Lewis and the Honeybears gave way to Aaron Lee Tasjan to provide a quality climax to Sunday and indeed the whole event.

For next year (pray it won't be necessary), I'd like to request virtual Modelos and Margaritas on tap. Apart from that omission, I was surprised and impressed by how successful and comprehensive the whole operation was.

BANDS SEEN IN 2021

Reverend Peyton's Big Damn Band
The Wandering Hearts
Belako
Alien Tango
Aiofe Nessa Frances
Pillow Queens
Chubby And The Gang
Penelope Isles
American Dreamer
Betty Soo
Como Las Movies
Sparks
Carson McHone The Deer
William Harries Graham
Jon Dee Graham
Black Joe Lewis and the Honeybears
Aaron Lee Tasjan

YEAR 19: 2022 / MARCH 15 - 19

Distilled from reviews in Record Collector,
Caught In The Act and Americana UK.

The trauma of sorting out all the paperwork leading up to departure climaxed with an intimidating procedure involving doing a Covid test on Zoom and then finding, on arrival at the airport, that the attestation I had carefully filled out on paper, as instructed, now had to be done online in a phone app in the queue for the check-in. However, I felt rather smug that I seemed to be not quite as inept as most of the people there, who had even less in the way of correct paperwork, and slightly relieved not to be among the baffled-looking phoneless pensioners for whom there were specially designated staff on duty.

On the plane, I found myself next to a most charming young musician, who oddly was also the proprietor of a very upmarket manufacturer of dressing gowns. He introduced me to his bandleader and also to another couple of performers. Julian and I synchronised simultaneous viewings of the new Bond film, only to be frustrated when it was switched off in the vital final five minutes because we were landing.

As I was in some doubt as to who I was actually going to go and see this year at South By Southwest, I decided to give my new friend's band a listen, as he was so charming. Trying to fit them, and indeed anything, into the schedule has been made considerably more difficult by the abolition of the incredibly useful little booklet that used to list every day's gigs in a logical order. Instead, you have to download an app, not much use on a phone like mine that doesn't work unless you go into somewhere and sign up to their Wi-Fi. This app does not present the gigs in a useful way. They're listed only by name of artist and name of venue. That is fine if you know the name of the artist or the venue you want to go to, but one of the greatest joys of South By Southwest is just having a look to see what's on and taking a chance on a name that sounds interesting. I decided to concentrate mainly on tried and trusted acts and do careful research to find when they were playing.

Each day your inbox is stuffed with upwards of fifty different pleading messages from managers, agents and record companies, trying to entice you to go and see their band and choose that particular option out of the hundreds that are available. Sometimes it's worth being just taken by a particular name in an email and trying to find out what they're actually like. Each message begins with a blatantly insincere enquiry as to the recipient's state of health and well-being, before listing some reasons why this particular act is far more important than any others playing at the same time. In actual fact, I did, during the course of the week, take blind steps in the dark occasionally, but mainly it was a matter of artists I already knew and recommendations from other people that I trusted.

The first night found us in a student satellite town called San Marcos, thirty miles outside Austin, spending the night in an Airbnb in a converted school bus in someone's backyard in a trailer park. It was quaint but I could have wrung the neck of the very persistent rooster who launched into song at 6 a.m. and kept going for three hours. San Marcos appealed to my romantic notions of Americana, as the mile-long lonesome-whistling trains clanked their mournful way across the main street.

The next day consisted of buying supplies from Walmart, having some breakfast in the ever-delightful Star Seeds cafe, checking into the pretty average (but well situated) hotel and taking the hire car back to the airport. From now on, because hire and petrol costs were so prohibitive, we were dependent on feet and public transport.

Having researched as much as we could with our inadequate tools, it was time to venture out into the musical maelstrom.

Musically, Tuesday was a classic South By Southwest day of ludicrous contrasts, shockingly terrible sound quality, bands of extraordinary variety, and far too much beer (which has also gone up enormously in price since last time around). The musical styles varied from something called Queer Country from Kentucky (S.G. Goodman, definitely an artist to watch) to some lamentable punk from Bristol (Grandma's House, who despite their admirable apostrophe, hadn't done sufficient rehearsing), and some atmospheric ambient desert sounds which were like a Pink Floyd album without the exciting bits (SUSS). The traditional up and coming acts like Yard Act were of course out in force, already drunk (who can blame them?) plus a band which I went from hating to adoring within 40 minutes, MELTS from Dublin. My new friend Julian from the aeroplane was backing the Irish poet Sinead O'Brien in one of his custom suits, the whole thing being inaudible on account of the shockingly incompetent sound engineer. We returned to the hotel by night bus, which broke down on the way. Switching on my phone very late (it didn't work anywhere other than in the hotel room) I received some very bad news about the health of Chuck Prophet. Sleep, brooding on the news, was fitful to say the least.

Knowing that the rest of the week was likely to be quite full and challenging, we decided to make Wednesday a less hectic affair. We ambled along to Lucy's Fried Chicken, SXSW's current home of Americana music, to enjoy laid-back lunchtime shows from Jesse Dayton and Darden Smith. Lucy's, despite having a spectacular line-up this year, is one of Austin's least suitable venues. It can't decide whether it's a restaurant or a music venue and the way it's set up tends to cause conflict. People arrive early and occupy the dining tables, which are behind a large space in front of the stage, but if anybody attempts to stand in front of the stage in order to see the bands, the customers sitting at the tables get in a rage and ask them to move. Therefore, unless the place is packed, there is usually a half moon of empty space on the gravel in front of the performing area. I stepped up to try and take a photo of Darden Smith and within seconds a red-faced and presumably red-necked gentleman was shoving me in the back and shouting out, "Are you going to f****** stand there blocking my view all day?" I wanted to say to him that he could at least have said, "Excuse me, would you mind moving?" but I didn't dare, simply slinking away timidly, before continuing down the road to the Hotel San Jose. Here there was considerably more space.

After two fallow Covid years, Paul and I had a lot to catch up on, so we sat on a bench on South Congress and nattered for a couple of hours in the hot sunshine before continuing, with increasingly agonizing blisters, to the Side Bar, a venue that represents everything that's authentic in Austin music. It's an absolutely filthy dive bar with disgusting toilets and a front room that has no lighting on the stage and sun streams through the windows behind the band so you can't see them. We certainly could hear the psychedelic tones of Gift and the post-Oasis indie of Enumclaw, before heading outside to be absolutely blown apart by the magnificent radical socialist roots rock of Alabama's Lee Bains III and the Glory Fires (for the third year running).

Being no longer able to walk, I begged Paul to hire some of those lethal scooters and by a miracle we arrived at Guero's with our lives intact. Indeed, after gallumphing the incomparably delicious enchiladas, several more beers and a couple of margaritas, we reboarded our scooters and swished through the dark side streets in a state that isn't recommended for someone like me, an old knackered twit in his mid-seventies. Time for bed, because it was going to be busy tomorrow.

Thursday saw a long trek to Lucy's to catch up with the Rubilators, whose Byrdsian jingle-jangle set was a tonic. Things have been hard for these guys. John Notarthomas has had to set himself up as a carpenter. "You don't know how good it feels to be back", said singer Walter Clevenger. "Oh yes we do!" shouted the audience back. Almost every artist made a point of saying how wonderful it felt to be returning to normality after the pandemic but not a single one (that we saw) made reference to the little matter of a war raging in Europe.

One dose of Lee Bains hadn't been enough, so we went back for more from the ultimate orator. If he was a politician in power, things would look a lot better for the world. A visit to the Cedar Street Courtyard didn't reveal much in the way of interesting music. The place had been taken over by the so-called British Embassy and filled with unexciting, over-subsidized bands. The evening, however, was well spent at the outstanding Mohawk venue, with two rooms accommodating more than a dozen acts of the kind of outstanding quality and variety you would expect from the 25th anniversary of the Bella Union label. Everyone was good, but to make a choice, the outstanding contributors, despite the presence of both Midlake and White Denim, were the extraordinarily gifted Penelope Isles and the joker in the pack, Pom Poko, an explosion of energy and fun from Norway. Ezra Furman was ill, so 83-year old trouper Ural Thomas calmly stepped up to play a second set. In case any of my family are reading this, I will draw a veil over the crazy and extremely dangerous route home, drunk on an electric scooter, negotiating busy highways and potholed pavements.

Friday was the day for checking out the new UK buzz bands, so we hopped on a delightfully cheap bus and pitched up at the Convention Center. The sumptuous environs of the ballroom allowed a good view, if you didn't happen to be behind one of the TV camera people. Wet Leg come from my part of the world and I found them highly entertaining and hard to classify, something that is of great merit in an industry often based on musical norms. Straight afterwards came Yard Act and, joy of joys, this time they were actually audible. Content wise, imagine a mixture of John Cooper Clarke, Pulp, Sleaford Mods, the Fall and John Shuttleworth and you have a truly great and innovative band. Both these bands will do well, although goodness knows what the Americans will make of buttered muffins and fixer-uppers.

Now it was time to attempt to get to somewhere several miles away with feet that were shot away with blisters. Dear friends, when you text me to say, "If you are in Austin you have to check out so-and-so", please bear in mind that it's not like a normal festival where you can just amble across a field. Slow progress took me all the way to Lucy's Fried Chicken, whose programmer must be a genius, because the quality of the musicians is so much better than the quality of the venue. There was no hope of getting near to any of the bands, so Susto was an audio experience only. A carefully-planned attempt to appreciate the Dream Syndicate properly was ruined by an 8-foot tall giant pushing in front of me and holding his recording device and phone above his head for the duration. In other words, I could see nothing, the crowd being so packed that there was nowhere to move to. Add in the fact that somebody stole my beer and I wasn't happy. It was possible to hear, though, that guitarist Jason Victor was one of the most innovative players of the week.

I am quite proud of the next bit. I had identified somewhere where we could hang out in relative comfort and peace. It was the premiere of a film about British folk music and it took place in a venue that was both spacious, quiet and comfortable. I had found out about it from my new friend Julian from the plane, but before he and Sinead O'Brien could appear, we had to view the film and listen to an hour of finger-in-the-ear folk performed by an ensemble of nine (count 'em) people who had been flown over from the UK, complete with their vintage instruments, to perform in front of a small bunch of their British musical friends. Whatever is this about? I'm not objecting to the music, which was fine except for adding nothing to the folk era in which I grew up (and which we later grew to scorn on account of its backward-looking incestuousness), but I'm still glad we went because there was ... yes, FREE BEER! We indulged copiously, as it would have been a shame to waste it.

Julian informed me that Sinead O'Brien had brought her own sound engineer, but it was still impossible to understand anything she was saying. The musical backing was great though, and much like SUSS had been Pink Floyd without the exciting bits, Sinead was PJ Harvey without the tunes. The bus tickets were still valid and we made it back with all the other deadbeats who ride the US public transport system. I felt quite at home.

On Saturday, ridiculous delights filled the afternoon at Lucy's, with a Big Star tribute featuring John Doe and Steve Wynn opening the programme. The bad news referred to on Day One was of course the illness of Chuck Prophet, so naturally the fans and followers, myself included, were out in force to express their support and care. In a burst of doctor-sanctioned gig activity, Chuck and the Mission Express were indulging in a typical SXSW string of shows, all of which we intended to catch. But before that, there was another bit of familiar SXSW-ism to be experienced - plodding a long distance to a show that you can't get into because it's sold out (in this case, Jesse Dayton and James McMurtry at the Continental). Silly idea in the first place.

At Lucy's, a show was taking place with the Continental Drifters supergroup, featuring Vicki Petersen of the Bangles, Susan Cowsill and Peter Holsapple. Excitement was high, moving to hysterical with the arrival of the Mission Express. Few artists inspire admiration and loyalty like Chuck, and the air was filled with emotion, a mixture of joy and sympathy. Now was the time for me to eat humble pie and stop dissing Lucy's, because despite not being able to see anything or be near the stage (old 8-foot tall bloke was in evidence again, causing bother) the atmosphere was so electric that the environment was irrelevant. The band members were beaming with nervous happiness and Chuck himself, despite a hint of frailty, was exploding with his usual energy and good humour. During Wish Me Luck, tears were flowing round the room as an audience initiative arranged for a surprise event in which everyone held up a paper plate with the song's title inscribed on it. One thing I knew (and I was right): Chuck would treat his recovery with the same determination as this performance and would be back.

Now things became even more surreal as we scootered to a house concert held in the garden of a multi-millionaire businessman, whose house was named The Castle. Indeed it was a castle, with a full stage in the garden. It felt like a scene out of some Netflix movie, as servants flitted discreetly around, firepits crackled beneath the uplit palm trees and, most worryingly, mysterious men in black suits sat in sinister groups, speaking an unidentified language. This was a rare outing for the Mission Express cabaret set (no You Did, but a sublime Summertime Thing), which was performed with good humour to an audience of largely disinterested non-music lovers. What an extraordinary experience.

Their third show of the evening was held down the road at C-Boys. Before we went in, we purchased some excellent falafels from an adjacent food truck. As we ate, the sound of the Continental Drifters performing Meet On The Ledge simply added to the madness. On the minuscule stage, Chuck and the Mission Express, seemingly indefatigable, laid waste to a wild audience, climaxing with a mind-boggling version of Willie Mays Is Up At Bat featuring Charlie Sexton on third guitar. Seldom has any musical experience ever felt so intense.

Well, after every high will inevitably come a low. My wife told me before I left that I'd come back with Covid, and she was right. Was it worth it? Of course!

BANDS SEEN IN 2022

Lee Bains III & The Glory Fires
Big Joanie
The Continental Drifters
Jesse Dayton
John Doe
The Dream Syndicate
Enumclaw
Gift
S.G. Goodman
Grandma's House
Penelope Isles
Ida Mae
MELTS

Midlake
Sinead O'Brien
Pom Poko
Chuck Prophet & The Mission Express
The Rubilators
Darden Smith
SUSS
Susto
Ural Thomas & The Pain
Wet Leg
White Denim
Steve Wynn
Yard Act

YEAR 20: 2023 / MARCH 14 - 18

Distilled from reviews in Record Collector,
Caught In The Act and Americana UK.

The Zombies dominated the entire week, with three live performances promoting their new album Different Game and the première of their new biopic Hung Up On A Dream. An acoustic duo show at Waterloo Records from Colin Blunstone and Rod Argent melted hearts and minds with the beauty and sincerity of their music, while viewers of the film became quite emotional as unexpected details of the band's history were revealed. They also performed two big outdoor shows, demonstrating that the American audience remains true to the band's heritage. The audiences were surprisingly young and even screams could be heard! The plushy confines of the Zach Theater hosted the première of their new feature-length documentary film Hung Up On A Dream. The undisputed star is Colin Blunstone, who comes across as hilariously affable as well as a vocal genius. One of his many anecdotes relates how, when Time Of The Season became a number one US hit after the band had split up, several fake Zombies bands started touring - one of them featuring two members of ZZ Top! Another great story from Colin was of the two-year period during which a record company changed his name to Neil Macarthur. Colin recalls walking down streets and thinking it was some kind of command when passers-by would shout out "Neil"!

On arrival, barely off the plane, we stumbled, without much

optimism, into a showcase at the Belmont Hotel by 75 year-old Doors guitarist Robbie Krieger. Would this be a shambolic affair from a washed-up old hippie? Far from it. With a series of guest Morrisons including actor Dennis Quaid and Robbie's son Waylon (looking like a Madchester refugee) they produced a panoramic ninety-minute Doors set that was so musically impeccable that it came close to experiencing the original band. The various substitute Manzareks on keys were all brilliant. This sort of thing only happens at SXSW.

While on the subject of heritage acts, surely one of the most unexpected names to be spotted in the copious SXSW listings was that of Dana Gillespie. The vivacious sixties icon had flown in her youthful bunch of virtuosos The London Blues Band, led by pianist Dino Baptiste, to promote her 73rd album (really) at the age of 73. To experience her strutting her blues stuff (including psychedelic spiritual chants) on the stage of the Continental Club was both surreal and endearing. A sixties survivor with a similar vibe to Marianne Faithfull, she held court charmingly at various venues around the city.

On to some garage rock. The Courettes were making their US debut on a bill consisting mainly of Danish acts presented by the Crunchy Frog label. Our disappointment at a food offering dominated by large amounts of meat was tempered by a wildly energetic performance by the Brazilian/Danish duo, hurling themselves round a rather demure restaurant. I'm a big fan of twosomes like The Kills and the Black Keys that blast out bluesy power pop and rush around cheerfully. I think the States will take to them.

Just as they do each year, Alabama's Lee Bains III and the (new) Glory Fires rattled through eight shows in three days. They really have everything – soul, melody and a strong, good-natured political element. Introducing each song with a monologue pleading for justice and inclusivity gives an inspiring context and feels like (loud) poetry of the highest calibre.

Adam Weiner swore in 2019 that Low Cut Connie would never play another SXSW. Yet at C-Boy's he was declaring, in his inimitable way, undying affection for the event he has missed so much. The core of Adam and guitarist Will Donnelly remains solid while the rest of the band fluctuates. The current formation is outrageously - dare I say it - sexy, with the provocative onstage antics even wilder than before. "I love you", declares Adam after each song in his wife-beater vest from atop his upright piano, and it's reciprocated in spades.

Psych-style wig-outs are always a rewarding feature of SXSW and the most thrilling this year came from an unexpected source. After an increasingly rocking country set at a packed C-Boy's, Sarah Shook warned the audience to expect something different as the Disarmers launched into a distortion-ridden ten-minute slow instrumental dominated by heavily treated pedal steel. With the dark melody benefiting from increasingly intense repetition, Mogwai or My Bloody Valentine would have been proud of them.

I got Warmduscher wrong! With their reassuringly cosy name conjuring up summery images of warm showers, I had expectations of something maybe a bit Grandaddy-ish. Instead, they won the prize for the shoutiest band around other than Pigs x7, also playing round the corner. The Warmduscher show at Hotel Vegas was enlivened by the despairing bassist's mic not being switched on for the entire set and then his instrument packing up, forcing him to borrow a bass from Dream Wife. There's definitely a market for this loud, heavy stuff (much heavier than their album) and they made up for the absence of And You Will Know Us By The Trail Of Dead.

At High Noon, the atmosphere was edgy and the banter from James Patrelli increasingly deranged as we accustomed ourselves to the newest (completely reconfigured) version of White Denim. The duelling guitarists are a crazed amalgam of Wishbone Ash and John McLaughlin as they smack out their jazzy octaves at ridiculous speed. It's hugely impressive yet somehow baffling as Patrelli confrontationally goads the audience, reminding them that he's been doing this for 18 years. Yes, one can definitely get too much guitar noodling, but the intensity made for a memorable experience.

Austin was full of German bands for the week and one called

GEWALT caught my attention by emailing me direct and citing one of their influences as Sleaford Mods, who also endorse them. It was a classic SXSW scenario with a gaggle of German bands playing to each other (and no one else) on the front porch of a grocery store in the outskirts. I thought I'd seen everything in rock and roll but nothing prepared me for vocalist Patrick Wagner, whose tortured spasms of jerky movement would put Lee Brilleaux to shame. Spattering sweat everywhere and seemingly almost out of control, at one stage he unzipped his flies and reached in, before pulling back from a Morrison moment that would have got him arrested in seconds in Texas. The industrial-style music was so powerful that this is the trio that would, for me, answer the annual question, "Which was the nost memorable band you saw this year?"

Although Jane Weaver has played at SXSW before, in 2016, her shows this time definitely had the feel of an attempted US launch. The success was questionable because the Central Presbyterian Church was barely half full, but her performance at the age of 51 was stunning, one of the standout memories of the week. The unfortunate tag 'folktronica' doesn't do her gorgeous melodies, ethereal tones, deafening volume, graceful stage presence and outstanding backing band enough justice.

Choosing exactly who to go and see at SXSW is always a challenge. This year I decided to go for names that meant something to me. Top picks were English Teacher (because I used to be one), Their/They're/There (because of my grammar fixation) and Dream Wife (because I have one). It didn't go too well, because we failed to find Their/They're/There and English Teacher were so bland that I can't remember anything about them. Dream Wife were fabulous though, a completely up-for-it young quartet having the time of their lives with their captivatingly cheerful / angry pop-rock and energetic stage antics.

As usual, I found much of the British presence at SXSW embarrassing. There has always been the tradition of scores of UK bands travelling to Texas to play to each other and now they have taken over one of Austin's finest venues and turned it into Little

Britain. Big walls have been built around the entrance to the Cedar Street Courtyard to emphasise the separateness, while inside all the UK musicians and industry types allow themselves to be royally ripped off by the clever Austinites, who charge them ten dollars for a small beer - by far the dearest anywhere in the city. Often sponsored by unsuspecting UK taxpayers (I found myself staring at a LED screen advertising Belfast City Council), it's true to say that each year one or two bands will achieve a breakthrough here, while many, many more will return home disappointed. We'd never heard of Prima Queen, who are based in London with an American singer from Chicago, but they were pleasingly melodic and characterful enough to give them a solid chance.

A gritty test for any UK band is to take their music to the US heartlands and see how they get on. Thus it was that Brighton's The Heavy Heavy were taken to the Texans' hearts at Hotel San Jose and went down a storm with their Fleetwood Mac-ish image and west coast sounds. It's certainly possible for a UK band to sustain a US career - just look at Skinny Lister. The Heavy Heavy's chances are better than even.

I'm always on the search for true Americana. If you aren't going to find it in Texas, where else? As the discussions meander on about what Americana is, we know that we can't define it but we sure know it when we hear it. And there are plenty of customers who attend SXSW and only listen to Americana-style bands. The mighty Canadian Six Shooter label has come a long way from the wild days of their annual hootenannies and now they have huge acts like The Dead South on their books. They have always had a great ear for new artists and the soothingly sincere tones of fast-rising William Prince made for a pleasant start to the day at Swan Dive. The tacos and Margaritas weren't bad either.

Stumbling on something brilliant when you least expect it is one of the joys of SXSW. Feeling badly let down by a performance by Nude Party that verged on the amateurish, I headed for the Continental Club to catch Jon Dee Graham, to be confronted by the depressing sight of a static queue and House Full signs. There was nothing for it but to dive into the adjacent Goorin's Hat Shop, where the outstanding honky-tonk sounds of Tender Things had inspired a mass outbreak of two-stepping. Describing themselves as a 'hippie country' band, they are led by Jesse Ebaugh, formerly of Heartless Bastards. As the loping groove became more and more overpowering, the feeling was "Yes! This is Americana!" An honourable mention also goes to David Wax Museum, whose mutant prog Tex-Mex slayed the Continental Club the following day.

When I look back on SXSW 2023, Daniel Romano's Outfit is the experience I will remember most clearly. Looking like a young Peter Green in his stylish leather jacket, Daniel exudes effortless cool throughout. Actually, at the C-Boy's outside show it's three bands, as the revue-style 90-minute show features three dovetailing sets, first by fast-rising singer Juliana Riolino, then Romano's wife Carson McHone who, if there's any justice, will follow Courtney Marie Andrews as the next major break-through Americana artist. By the time the downbeat but charismatic Romano takes centre stage (and later to the drums), Riolino has turned into a dervish-like, stage-rolling, beer-swilling rocker and the entertainment factor has reached fever pitch. Simply brilliant.

BANDS SEEN IN 2023

Lee Bains III & The Glory Fires
Charlotte Rose Benjamin
The Bright Light Social Hour
Brooke Combs
The Courettes
David Wax Museum
Dream Wife
Gewalt
Giddy Up Go
Dana Gillespie
Gypsy Mitchell

The Heavy Heavy
Jenifer Jackson with Jon Notarthomas
The Adam Johnson Band
Robby Krieger
Low Cut Connie
Manta Rays
Carson McHone
Nude Party
Prima Queen
William Prince
Chuck Prophet & The Mission Express
Red Rum Club
Juliana Riolino
Daniel Romano's Outfit
Ron Gallo
Sarah Shook & The Disarmers
The Tender Things
The Texas Gentlemen
Thee Sacred Souls
Jeff Tweedy
Warmduscher
Jane Weaver
White Denim
The Zombies

TWENTY-ONE

There's something about that number. It's not what you would call a 'round number' but somehow it has tremendous significance. I guess nowadays that 18 is more important for people growing up, but when I was young, 21 was the important benchmark for adulthood. That's why I originally planned to document 21 Years Of South By Southwest.

What is it about 21? It's referred to as 'coming of age', but what happened to me in attempting to reach 21 years of SXSW was the coming of another type of age altogether, namely old age. In September I'd celebrated my 75th birthday and somehow felt that I had just about got away with being old but still rocking and rolling without appearing too ludicrous. My favourite band, with which I began this book, the Hollies, were still touring and my 75th birthday present from my wife was to go and see them, and indeed interview them and photograph them for Record Collector. They still seemed cool and I certainly felt a lot younger than most of their audience, so I had absolutely no doubts about the plan to head back to Austin as usual in March 2024.

Unfortunately, fate had other plans, because somehow I picked up a very debilitating and frightening virus and, as the day for flying to Texas grew nearer, I began to realize that the copious antibiotics prescribed by my GP were not doing the trick and that it would be foolish to attempt to fly. Two of the main symptoms of the virus were extended coughing fits and vomiting, neither of which would be compatible with a ten-and-a-half hour flight. I've sat next to people like that on planes before and it's unbearable. The time therefore came for me to confess to Paul that I was not going to be able to make it, followed by a programme of flight and hotel cancellations and a sick feeling of intense frustration and disappointment.

I lay on the sofa feeling sorry for myself for five days, reading Paul's bulletins from a quite clearly vibrant and brilliant South By Southwest 2024. Unwittingly, I was handing over the baton to Paul, because he cheerfully took on the task of documenting the festival in words and pictures for the various outlets expecting reports from me. That's why this book is subtitled 20 years of SXSW, rather than 21.

But still I felt guilty at abandoning Paul. Our SXSW 'journey' had always been carried out as a partnership. I'd taken him and his goodwill for granted. For years, he'd driven us around from venue to venue without ever a complaint. He'd put up with my fawning and my never-ending paranoia at having to cover the most prestigious shows and create a strong impression for the powers-that-be. But what's this now? I'm reading the review that I demanded that Paul write in my absence and, guess what, it's a lot better than I would have managed. When I first met Paul, I was the one doing the reviewing. Remember the precision of the equipment listing and the impeccably neat handwriting? Now it turned out that Paul was a journalist in waiting, and I was thrilled.

The first day of my home confinement saw the announcements of the deaths of two of my favourite musicians, Malcolm Holcombe and Karl Wallinger of World Party. Both had cheated death before - Wallinger had a brain aneurism in 2001, yet was back performing at SXSW in 2006. So not everyone is Keef-style indestructible and maybe all this is a warning.

But who knows? There's always next year. Maybe it'll be the best SXSW ever?

PS. I was NOT asleep!

Also by Oliver Gray:

VOLUME
A cautionary tale of rock and roll obsession

V.A.C.A.T.I.O.N.
Cautionary tales of travelling without style

ALAB (with Eddie Hardin)
35 years of musical mayhem on the road with
the Spencer Davis Group

ACCESS ONE STEP
The official history of the Joiner's Arms

ZANDER
An Americana whodunnit

BANJO ON MY KNEE
A musical journey through the American south

POLLY IN MY POCKET
Cautionary tales of camper van life

DETENTION
Cautionary tales from the world of education

All published by Sarsen Press, Winchester, UK